D1420708

# ATLANTIC
# QUEENS

# ATLANTIC QUEENS

CLIVE BROOKS

To Rosemary Bromley for making my career sail forwards at a rate of knots, and to Pat and Eric Moody for the insight into a potential new lifestyle!

**A FOULIS Boating Book**

First published 1989


Published by:
**Haynes Publishing Group**
Sparkford, Near Yeovil, Somerset
BA22 7JJ, England

**Haynes Publications Inc.**
861 Lawrence Drive, Newbury Park,
California 91320, USA

**British Library Cataloguing in Publication Data**
Brooks, Clive
Atlantic Queens
1. Passenger transport. Shipping. Steam liners. (Ship) Queen Mary, (Ship) Queen Elizabeth, (Ship) Queen Elizabeth 2, history. (Ship) Queen Mary, history. (Ship) Queen Elizabeth, history. (Ship) Queen Elizabeth 2, history
I. Title
387.2'432
ISBN 0 85429 639 5

**Library of Congress Catalog Card Number**
89-84298

Editor: Peter Johnson
Page layout and design: Phil Lyons

Printed in England by:
J.H. Haynes & Co. Ltd.

# Contents

# Acknowledgements

Considerable thanks are firstly due to Peter Boyd-Smith of Cobwebs Ocean Liners Souvenir store in Southampton for all the assistance given in the compiling of this book. He has kindly lent considerable rare and valuable materials that are unavailable elsewhere, making this publication extremely unique. In addition, he has directed me to acquaintances who have been able to furnish me with further excellent visual materials.

Cobwebs is unique, being the only shop of its kind in the world. The maritime section started from a shoebox in 1979 and by 1986 had grown into a thriving business housed in a Victorian shop on several floors. The store has been featured extensively in major publications and national media on both sides of the Atlantic and many of the major television companies rely on Peter for period items for use in maritime productions.

Recently Peter has been providing Cunard with a display cabinet on board QE2 where some of his unique china, silverplate, posters, postcards and period publications can be viewed and bought by passengers. He is often interested in purchasing maritime items and can be contacted on (0703) 227458.

I would also like to extend grateful thanks to Terry Holmes, George & Joan Caws, Mitch Caws, Tom Grant, Ron Macey, Peter Indge, Pam Savory, Bob Coles, Harley Crossley, Bill Winberg at the Queen Mary Hotel in Long Beach, California, Phil Small, Maurice Barnes, Cliff Moore for his guided tour of QE2, Robin Davies, Eric Flounders and Helen Heynes in the Cunard PR office, Platou Ship Design, John Edgar Mann (alias Tom Bargate), Rod Grainger, Rosemary Bromley, Peggy Brooks, and everyone else who has assisted me in the preparation of this book.

Photographs are credited with each caption. My thanks to all the photographers, present and past, as well as to the few whose names are not known.

# I
# Ocean Palaces

The Queen Mary, Queen Elizabeth and QE2 come from a long and distinguished nautical family that stretches back over almost one hundred and fifty years. By 1839, Samuel Cunard of Halifax, Nova Scotia, was already a successful businessman and founder of the Quebec and Halifax Steam Navigation Company. Six years earlier, the line's steamship, Royal William, made one of the first Atlantic steam crossings; until then, vessels had relied upon the power of the winds alone.

Mr Cunard travelled with a letter of introduction from the Governor General of Nova Scotia, to England where he met the secretary of the Admiralty, Charles Wood. He made a formal bid for a contract to carry mail across the ocean, and was awarded it on May 4, 1839. It was to run for a period of ten years, in which Cunard was required to operate three ships. For this service, he was offered £55,000 per year.

After securing the contract, Cunard was introduced to Scottish shipbuilder Robert Napier. Napier managed to persuade Samuel Cunard to build bigger ships than those specified by the contract, and also to commission four instead of three vessels. The price for each came to £30,000. An agreement was made with several other Scotsmen, who together could provide the necessary additional finance. The result was the North American Royal Mail Steam Packet Company, and £270,000 in capital. Samuel Cunard had put up the largest amount, his £55,000, and so therefore, the line duly became known as the Cunard Line.

Soon Cunard was back at the negotiating table, persuading the Admiralty to go for even larger ships, and for the service to be extended on to Boston from Halifax. His success in the matter, and the subsequent signing of a new contract on July 4, 1839, brought in a further subsidy which raised his annual income to £60,000. The first ship completed was the Britannia, which made her maiden voyage on July 4, 1840. She was a paddle steamer of 1,135 tons, 207 feet long, 34 feet wide, and with a service speed of nine knots. There was accommodation for 115 passengers, and space to convey 225 tons of cargo. Britannia's first voyage took twelve days and ten hours from Liverpool to Halifax, and then a further forty-six hours for the extension round to Boston. From the beginning, rules and regulations were Cunard's hallmarks. The staterooms were to be swept every morning, beginning at 5 am. Slops were to be emptied discreetly while passengers were at breakfast, and thrown overboard on the leeward side to avoid the wind carrying them back into the vessel, and bed linens were to be changed every eight days. Even the passengers had strict rules, and were told to keep their scuttles shut and to extinguish the candles in their staterooms by midnight. However, they were pleased to find the wine and spirits bar open each morning from 6 am. On the Britannia's first arrival in Boston, Samuel

***The large, ornate silver vase presented to Samuel Cunard on Britannia's first arrival in Boston (Author photo)***

Cunard was presented with a large ornate silver vase, engraved with a commemorative inscription. It now occupies a prime site in one of the restaurants on board the Queen Elizabeth 2.

Charles Dickens took a passage to America on the Britannia early in January 1842, to give dramatic readings of his works, to lecture, and to try to do something about the lack of international copyright which had deprived him of all the revenue that his books had earned in the States. Cunard soon began to wish that he hadn't travelled with the line at all, as he soon penned a less-than-complimentary account of his experiences. When he saw his stateroom, he apparently described it as "an utterly impractical, thoroughly hopeless, and profoundly preposterous box!" He maintained that his bunk was a kind of shelf with a thin mattress covered, "like surgical plaster", by a flat quilt. "Nothing smaller for sleeping in was ever made except coffins", he claimed. The chance of his wife's luggage fitting into the cramped cabin was, he is reported to have said, "to be as remote as the possibility that a giraffe could be persuaded into a flower pot".

Dickens had seen an artist's impression of the saloon on board, and remembered the drawing as "a chamber of almost interminable perspective, furnished in a style of Eastern splendour." When he saw it himself, he is reported to have changed his opinion and called it "a hearse with windows". However, notwithstanding these singular criticisms, the Britannia was a tremendous success, and paved the way for a whole family of Cunard ships.

The other three ships, built to fulfil the mail contract were named the Arcadia, Caledonia and Columbia. Together with Britannia, these ships provided a fortnightly sailing from Liverpool between March and October, and a monthly service during the winter. The fares quoted were 34 guineas to Halifax, and 38 guineas to Boston.

Around this time, the Admiralty was again contacted. This time, Cunard managed to persuade them to increase their subsidy to £81,000. They agreed as long as another ship was built. This was duly arranged, and the fifth ship, christened the Hibernia, entered service on April 18, 1843. Until then, there had been no major misfortunes, but Cunard suffered a setback when the Columbia ran aground in fog on Seal Island near Cape Sable. The passengers were all safely transferred, but the Columbia was destined to become a total loss. This forced a replacement called the Cambria.

The Admiralty were obviously pleased with the service that Cunard was running, and consequently, by 1847, they had awarded a further contact, this time to extend the mail service on to New York. This meant a further subsidy increase, to £156,000, over £100,000 more than the original agreement. For this extra capital, Cunard was required to provide a weekly service throughout the summer, and a fortnightly one in winter. To ensure that the revised schedule could be met, four new paddle-steamers were ordered. These new ships, completed in 1848, were the largest yet, being 251 feet long, 38 feet wide, and weighing in at just over 1,800 tons. Their names: the America, Niagra, Europa and Canada.

With these new vessels in commission, Cunard had no further use for the old Britannia and Arcadia, and so they were sold to the German Confederation Navy. Cunard felt that six vessels would be adequate to maintain his schedules, especially in view of the fact that average speeds had already increased from nine to twelve knots.

The Cunard Line was enjoying an enviable reputation, especially for safety, as it had not lost one single passenger. Samuel's instructions to his captains to avoid racing rival lines was a major contributing factor to this record, and was reflected in the company motto "speed, comfort and safety". The main rival was the New York and Liverpool United States Mail Steamship Company. This was commonly known as the Collins Line, after Edward Knight Collins, the founder. Collins ships were bigger and faster than Cunard's, and they had secured the lucrative U.S. mail contract with a subsidy of $385,000. By 1850, Collins Line was taking the largest percentage of the passenger traffic across the Atlantic. Cunard, on realizing this, managed to come to an agreement with Collins which guaranteed him one third of the trade. This was acceptable to Collins, as it provided him with a guaranteed income to cover his rapidly escalating operating expenses. All was well until Collins Line lost one of its ships, the Arctic. The vessel was involved in a collision off Cape Race, resulting in the loss of the ship and over 300 lives. The misfortune continued when, in January 1856, the Pacific sailed from Liverpool and was never heard from again. Because of these disasters, Collins was forced to discontinue operations in 1858. This was totally unexpected, and Samuel Cunard had been working hard to counter Collins superiority, building their first iron-hulled paddle steamer, called Persia. This vessel was 376 feet long, and 3,300 tons. It captured the Atlantic record in 1856 with a speed of 13.47 knots, a crossing of less than nine and a half days.

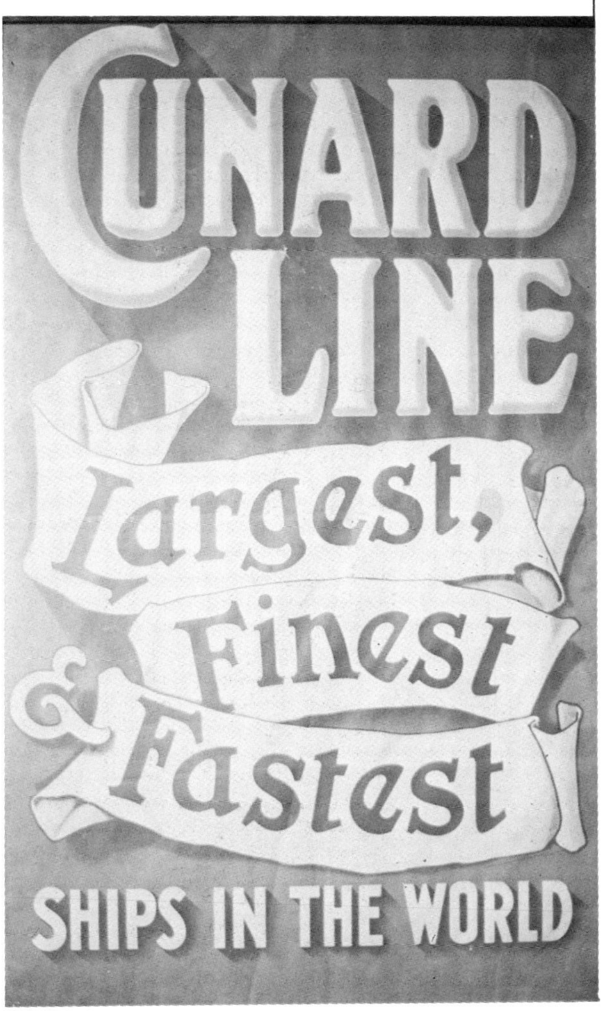


***Cunard publicity poster, c. 1900, reflecting the company motto (Author photo of Cobwebs collection)***

Cunard was determined to expand, and was operating a steamship service to the Mediterranean, running as far as Istanbul. In addition to this, he also began an emigrant service to the States when the Civil War ended, with eight new 1,800 tonners. However, his next principal project was the Scotia, built in 1862. This was to be the last of Cunard's paddle steamers. The China, which came next, relied on propellers to drive her, and weighed 2,638 tons. Following the success of this design departure, a similar vessel, named the Russia, was built.

On April 28, 1865, Samuel Cunard died. He was 78, and had been awarded a baronetcy by Queen Victoria in 1858 for his services to commerce, and also for the use of his ships in both the Crimea (1853-1856), and the Indian Mutiny of 1857. In his last fifteen years, he had seen a large increase in the amount of competing transatlantic companies; European based outfits had come into existence in addition to the American Line in the U.S.A. To make matters worse, Cunard had lost the Blue Riband, the coveted award for being fastest across the Atlantic, which it had held for thirteen years, to the Inman line, in 1869. Another source of pressure was the fact that White Star Line had set up a Liverpool to New York service, using ships that were frankly much better than Cunard's. To compete, Cunard upgraded their existing ships, and commissioned two further vessels, the Bothnia in 1874, and the Sythia in 1875. Unfortunately, neither could keep pace with White Star's Oceanic of 1871.

This resulted in Cunard going public, leading to the formation of the Cunard Steamship Company in 1878. With the resultant extra capital, the 7,392 ton Servia was built. This steel ship had a service speed of 16 knots. Space was available for 480 first class passengers, in addition to 750 places for steerage — the cheap carriage of emigrants that was becoming increasingly important to all the transatlantic companies. She was designed to lure back many of the customers that Cunard had lost in recent years, in a way of luxury forced on Cunard by its competitors. The Servia had five decks, a saloon with the grandest staircase on the Atlantic, and columns fluted and girded in a chaste style. Some of the staterooms were fitted with lavatories, something unheard of at the time! More well-equipped ships followed, but it was with the Aurania, launched in 1883, that Cunard came closest to disaster. Her engines exploded on her maiden voyage whilst in mid-Atlantic, forcing the continuance of the journey under sail. Thankfully, there was no loss of life.

After dealing with the Aurania's problems, Cunard Line were faced with another obstacle. They had recently taken over the liner Oregon from her struggling owners. The Oregon was a beautiful ship, elegant and majestic with a grand saloon that glowed from the light filtered through a dome of coloured glasses twenty feet high. The floors were parquet, and there were panels of polished satin-wood, pilasters of walnut with capitals of gilt. The ceilings were white and gold, and there was even a barber's shop on board with two luxurious American shaving chairs and hairbrushing machinery overhead. The Oregon had won back the Blue Riband for Cunard with an average speed of 18.39 knots, and her future looked assured. This was all to change when, on March 14, 1886, she collided with a sailing vessel near Long Island and sank. It was in the early morning when she was nearing Fire Island Light with 896 passengers and crew aboard. A schooner came silently out of nowhere, pierced the Oregon's bow and then disappeared again. The schooner's name was never learned, but the collision proved fatal. A large hole was ripped in the Oregon's side between her two boiler rooms. The Captain ordered the watertight doors closed, but accumulated coal dust on the sills had rendered them inoperative. The Oregon began to fill very slowly, and there was plenty of time to evacuate all passengers before she sank.

Cunard maintained the New York to Liverpool service with the Servia, Aurania, and two new ships, the Umbria of 7,718 tons (November 1884) and the Etruria (April 1885). Sails were becoming history, and already looked distinctly inadequate on a vessel of almost 8,000 tons. One officer said at the time that mechanical confidence had gone too far when they were discarded completely. He was proved right when the Umbria broke her shaft in mid-ocean and wallowed about helplessly for days. The Etruria soon found herself in similar circumstances, when the rudder and propeller dropped off. Cunard learnt its lesson, and the Etruria and Umbria were to be the last of the line's single-screw ships. For all their faults, the two sister ships did enjoy successful years, and included some unique innovations. Ice-rooms had been replaced by refrigerating machinery, the first ever installed on Atlantic liners, electric light was available, and there were pipe organs in the music rooms. Some of the staterooms were laid out en-suite, and they all featured a hot water heater, an electric light, and a life-saving cork jacket. Each ship had thirteen marble baths fitted with steam and shower apparatus. In addition, ladies could while away the time in a boudoir that formed a vestibule which led on to a whole series of scented baths and mirrored lavatories.

Following these ships, Cunard ordered the Campania of 12,950 tons, together with the Lucania. These were twin-screw ships, powered by five cylinder, triple expansion engines, and were the ultimate in luxury, often averaging over 21 knots. The interior chambers of these ships were grand and full of sculptured wood, stained glass and classic upholsteries: the Americans loved them. The design

***RMS Lucania (Author photo of Cobwebs collection)***

brief was that the vessels should be installed with everything that was currently fashionable on land, so that the cream of Victorian society could travel in the comfort, security and familiar decor of their own rooms. The following is an account of the ladies saloon on the Campania: "It is a charming retreat, the carpets are of a very pretty pattern; the lounges are wide, the cushions impart an exquisite sensation of buoyancy, geraniums are blooming, and the mignonette is exhaling its sweetness. It is a club house and boudoir combined; if my lady has a nervous headache, or wishes to escape the advances of an ardent but obtrusive admirer, or if she wants to read in quiet, or to gossip, or to fritter her time away in *dolce far niente*, she steals in here, and here is sanctuary."

The smoking room of the Campania was impressive, with its coach roof and piazza arrangement of chairs along the sides. It had an open fire grate, a hearth with Persian tiles and an oriental rug in front of it. A grand piano together with an American organ stood on the Persian carpet of the drawing room, the forward end of which was an inglenook. Electric lamps in the shape of rosettes of beaten copper lit the reading room. The dining room could seat 450 people in revolving armchairs placed in rows beside the long tables. The room was lit by a vast crystal dome that covered a light-well that extended downwards through three decks. Staterooms were advertised as being lofty and well-ventilated, and featured "Hopkins triptic beds". These were made so that the upper bed would fold up against the bulkhead. For those for whom money was no object, there were suites of rooms fitted out in satinwood and mahogany, with parlour and bedroom. The former was fitted up with tables and chairs in the style of a lady's boudoir, the latter fitted with a brass bedstead and hanging wardrobe, all adding up, as Cunard put it at the time, to "a silent sermon in good taste".

The turn of the century heralded a new era in shipping, with the formation in the U.S.A. in 1902 of the International Mercantile Marine Corporation (I.M.M.), founded by the banker and

Covers from early Cunard passenger lists c. 1890 (Author photos of Cobwebs collection)

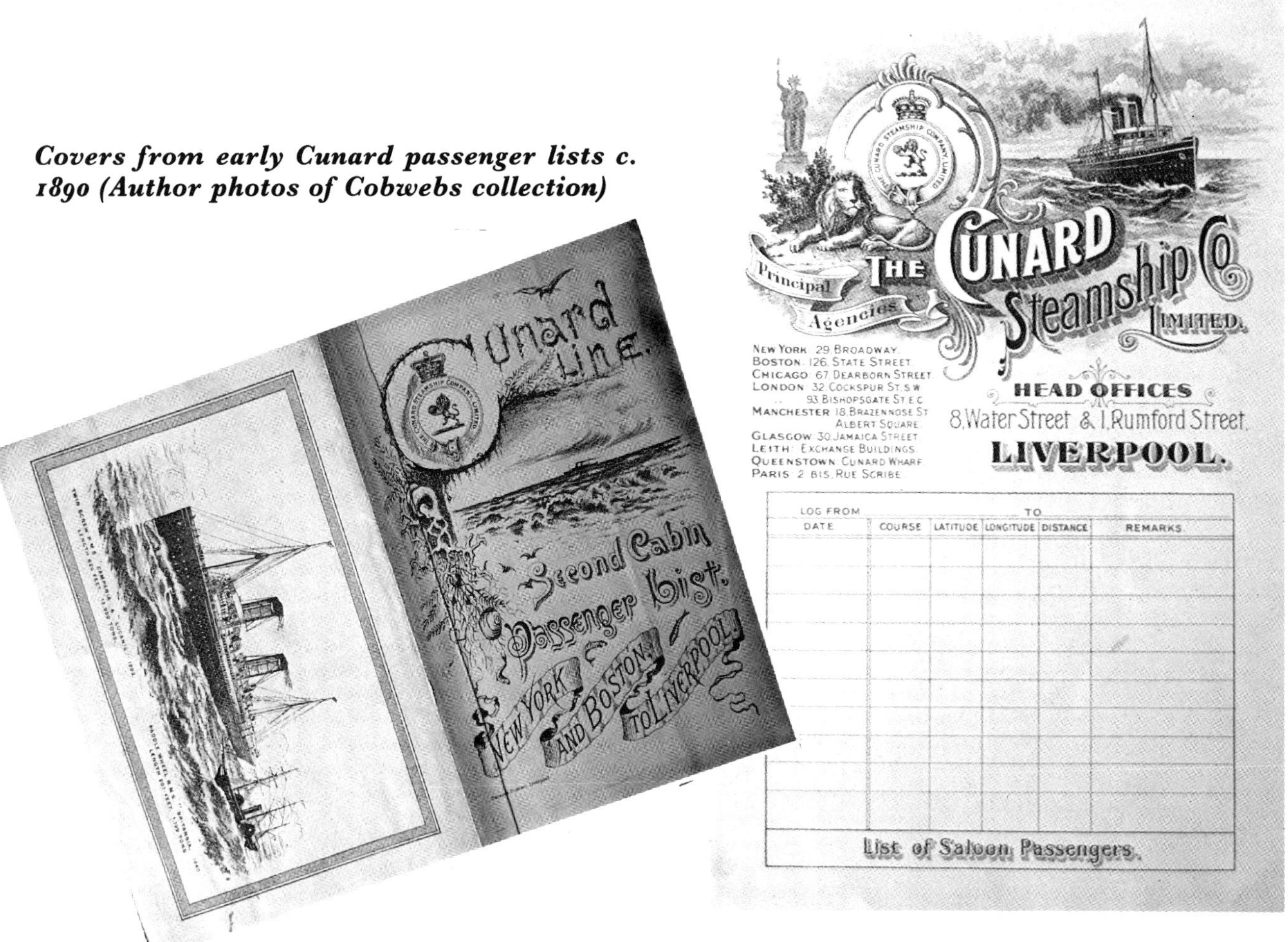


industrialist J.P. Morgan. He soon began taking over many shipping lines. Luckily, the British Government responded by assisting Cunard financially, enabling the line to build a pair of luxury superships for the Atlantic. The conditions were that Cunard would remain British, and that the ships would be available for use by the Admiralty whenever required. The first thing Cunard did was arrange the building of two ships, the Carmania and the Caronia. The first had Parsons steam turbines, whilst the latter was fitted with traditional reciprocating engines. The idea here was that different power plants could be compared before a final decision was made on powering the proposed superships. It turned out that Carmania was faster by about a knot for the same fuel consumption, and so turbines were chosen for the planned new ships.

John Brown on the Clyde was given the order to build one new vessel, the Lusitania, whilst Swan Hunter and Wigham Richardson on the Tyne set to work on the Mauretania. Once built, these two ships became the most famous Atlantic liners ever. Lusitania was the largest ship in the world when she entered service on September 7, 1907 (31,550 tons and 762 feet). In addition, she was also the fastest. In the same October, she achieved average speeds of just under 24 knots. However, she did have a few "teething" troubles to overcome when, after only four years in service, end-of-voyage reports mentioned fires caused by short circuits behind the panelling, started by rats who had gnawed through the rubber insulation.

The Mauretania's skin was constructed from steel plating of more than an inch thick. Some of these plates were fifty feet long and weighed over five tons each. Four million rivets were required to assemble the hull and superstructure of the ship. Special soft iron ones were used, and the yard had designed oil-fired wheeled furnaces which heated up huge quantities of them at a time. The engine to be used was a steam turbine, which at the time was very new and untried in a vessel of this size. It's application for marine use was made by a man called Charles Parsons. A jet of high pressure steam is brought to bear against a wheel rimmed with steel vanes. The beauty of this concept was that it had, in effect, only one moving part. There was supposed to be very little vibration, and the thunderous clatter of the traditional steam engine was replaced by a form of whine. The launch on a rainy September 20, 1906 featured a platform erected under the bows, with a toy capstan in the centre which would activate the release of hydraulic launching triggers. From the masthead on the bow hung a line tied securely around the neck of a bottle of champagne. This was concealed in ribbons and flowers, ready for the Dowager Duchess of Roxburghe, who had agreed to christen the ship. The launch party was led through three of Mauretania's funnels which lay on their sides, in an effort to further emphasise the new Cunarder's size. Cars could have passed through these, two abreast, with room to spare.

The Duchess was asked to turn the miniature capstan. For an instant, nothing happened, but after a few moments, the sixteen thousand tons of steel hull began to edge towards the water. The bottle of champagne was flung at the side of the ship where it smashed and dropped onto a workman's head! In the months that followed, Mauretania's superstructure took shape, and her new turbines were fitted. The cabins and public rooms for the first class passengers were located in the centre of the ship, and forward was a library, writing room and drawing room, the latter being designed as a solace for ladies who weren't welcome in the smoking room. There was a grand staircase which led down to the embarkation hall and dining room. Aft of this, the main lounge, the smoking room and finally, a verandah cafe. This was built with the hope of occasional fine weather on the New York run. Rush matting was laid on the deck, and potted palms and wicker furniture used to provide the illusion that you could sit outdoors. Cruising and sunbathing on deck was something for the future. The emphasis throughout the rest of the Mauretania was on constructing a cosy refuge from the treacherous seas outside.

Panelling was used extensively throughout the first class quarters; there was mahogany in the lounge, stairs and passages, maple in the drawing

***RMS Caronia (Cobwebs collection)***

***Lusitania was the largest ship in the world when she entered service on September 7 1907 (Author photo of Cobwebs collection)***

***Beautiful goblet made for the launching of the Mauretania 1906 (Cobwebs collections)***

room, walnut in the smoking room and weathered oak in the triple-decked dining room. There was a lot of feature carving too, of an incredibly high standard of workmanship. Three hundred craftsmen were brought over from Palestine and laboured for months. Some were so proud of their work that they initialled it. The panelling was installed with layers of felt insulating it from the steel of the ship to minimize any unwanted creaking. Thoughtful designs had been employed throughout; these included chandeliers which looked conventional, but would remain still whatever the ship's motion, plus cabin doors with special hooks fitted to hold them open in any position, however the ship pitched.

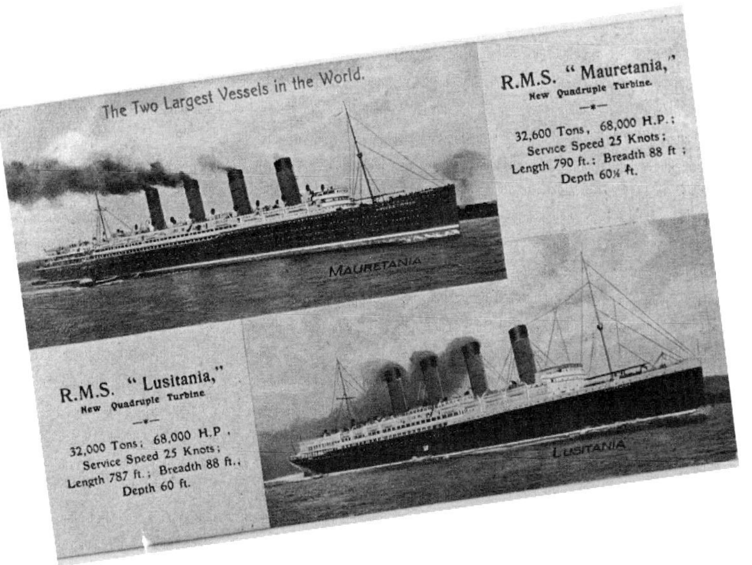


***Sister ships Mauretania and Lusitania (Author photo of Cobwebs collection)***

By late summer 1907, the panelling and lavish plaster ceilings were complete. Hundreds of swivel chairs were anchored to the deck, the staircases and lounges were carpeted in a soft green, while halls and passages were surfaced with traditional patterned rubber tiling. The appearance was perfect, but, on trials, a problem of vibration became apparent. This was so severe, that even those on the bridge, five hundred feet away from the propellers, were considerably shaken. Consequently, strengthening members were placed in the after sections, but new propellers had to wait a year, until one of the originals was lost at sea. The resulting new set reduced the vibrations significantly, and the Mauretania held the Blue Riband for twenty-two of her twenty-eight years in service.

In July 1921, the ship caught fire while tied up in Southampton. A man cleaning the carpets on E deck was smoking whilst using an inflammable liquid. The flash fire that took immediate hold sent clouds of dense black smoke through the ship. The fire crews directed their pumps at the ship, which began listing away from the pier. Mauretania was saved by a gang of men who worked under nine feet of water to release the catches on a starboard entry port to allow the excess water to drain out and alleviate the danger of a capsize. Towards the end of her life, the Mauretania was painted white and acted as a West Indian cruise ship with temporary canvas swimming pools installed on deck. When the ship did eventually come to "death row" — Southampton's Berth 108 — she had been in service for almost twenty-seven years. An auction was held for the ship's fixtures and fittings. When she sailed for the breakers in Scotland, crowds lined the shores, and a blue Riband with the legend 1907-1929 fluttered in the breeze from her masthead.

During the Mauretania and Lusitania's reign, Cunard's Lucania caught fire whilst docked in Liverpool in 1909 and was a total loss. For this reason, Cunard ordered another big ship, to be called the Aquitania. This was to be the last of the Cunard four-funnelled liners, and was dubbed the "ship beautiful". She was 45,647 tons, and looked similar to the Lusitania and Mauretania, except that she was given an extra deck, allowing her to carry 1,000 more passengers.

The new vessel featured the ultimate in interior decoration. For example, the lunettes in the first class drawing room were made in the same way as the lead lights placed over the front door of many London houses. If money was no object, then there was a choice of accommodation in a number of suites that took their cue from the painters after which they were named: Holbein, Gainsborough, Romney, Raeburn, Reynolds, Rembrandt, Van Dyck and Velasquez. Pompeiian and Turkish baths were provided on board, and there was a Garden Lounge. The walls of this were covered on one side with trellises and stone, and the setting was designed to give the feeling that you were in a chamber of the Palace of Versailles, looking onto the park of the Grand Trianon, with the palace itself being visible in the distance through a colonnade of flower-covered Doric columns. Walls were hung with blue tabourette silk onto which mezzotint portraits of eighteenth century court favourites were fixed.

Daylight on the ship was given to a double rank of inside cabins by a platform on the inboard side of the promenade deck. It not only raised occupants' deck chairs conveniently high enough to see over the rail, but also left space, within the riser, for a six-inch clerestory window into the cabin directly below. A similar window in the wall immediately behind the chair provided light for a cabin even further inside. However, not everyone agreed with the palatial effects; Arthur Davis, addressing colleagues at the Royal Institute of British Architects: "I said to the directors 'why don't you make a ship look like a ship?' The answer I was given was that the people who use these ships are not pirates, they do not dance hornpipes; they are mostly seasick American ladies, and the one thing they want to forget when they are on the vessel is that they are on a ship at all. Most of them have got to travel, and they object to it very much. In order to impress that point upon me, the company sent me across the Atlantic. The first day out I enjoyed the beautiful sea, but when we got well on to the Atlantic, there was one thing I craved for as never before, and that was a warm fire and a pink shade. The people who travel on these large ships are the people who live in hotels; they are not ships for sailors or yachtsmen or people who enjoy the sea. They are inhabited by all sorts of people, some of whom are very delicate and stay in their cabin during the whole voyage. I suggest to you that the transatlantic liner is not merely a ship, she is a floating town with 3,000 passengers of all kinds, with all sorts of tastes, and those who enjoy being there are distinctly in the minority. If we could get ships to look like ships, and get people to enjoy the sea, it would be a very good thing; but all we can do, as things are, is to give them gigantic floating hotels."

War came in 1914, and it wasn't long before all of Cunard's ships became involved. On May 15, 1915, the Lusitania was torpedoed off the Irish coast, sinking with a loss of 1,198 lives. On the fateful day, Captain William Turner wasn't steering the recommended zig zag course, and no one had bothered about a small black-framed notice that was inserted in the New York papers by the German Embassy in Washington, warning American passengers on British vessels that they were liable to attack. The weather was clear and warm, and the stewards had opened the portholes in the dining room, an act that was to prove fatal when a torpedo struck amidships. Extra time afforded by the closed watertight compartments was cancelled out by the number of open portholes on D deck and below.

Meanwhile, the Aquitania was requisitioned as an armed merchant cruiser, then converted, along

***The Mauretania and Lusitania were undoubtedly the 'super' ships of their time and here the Lusitania can be seen passing the earlier and smaller Caronia (Author photo of Cobwebs collection)***

***There were several ways to pay (Author photo of Cobwebs collection)***

with the Mauretania, to carry troops to the campaign in the Dardanelles. Following this, they became hospital ships, painted white with buff coloured funnels, and giant red crosses on their sides. Afterwards they returned once more to trooping duties from Canada to Europe. When the conflict ended, both ships resumed their commercial service.

To make up for the unfortunate loss of the Lusitania, Cunard took over the German liner Imperator. She was renamed the Berengaria, and allowed the Line to resume its transatlantic express service into the thirties. Shortly after the Berengaria was put into service, stability problems became apparent. Two days out of Cherbourg on her second voyage under the British flag, seawater poured into the ash ejectors and clogged the pumps. Several coaling ports leaked, and water rose in the bilges making the ship list critically. This caused the exodus of hundreds of rats from their lairs, who over-ran the ship. Eventually, access to the bilges was achieved by breaking through the tank tops and pumping out from above. When the ship reached Southampton, passengers were disgusted and told the press. The bad news perpetuated and culminated in questions being voiced in the House of Commons. Cunard announced that the ship's after funnel would be removed in a drastic bid to improve stability. In the event, this was never carried out. Instead, several other changes were made, including the removal of all marble bathtubs in the first-class suites, and the addition of one thousand tons of pig-iron to act as permanent ballast.

Staterooms were the parts of the ship that most passengers had lasting impressions of, and shipping lines endeavoured to make the limited space allocated to each passenger as attractive as possible.

But not everyone liked this approach. Siegfried Sassoon, the English poet, in a cheap cabin on the Berengaria: "I like it — this creaking, heaving, vibrating, white polished box — Mischa Elman's cabin was quite close to mine and I often heard him playing — The memory of those evening hours had a strange serenity; the drone and thud of the turbines, the pad and patter of feet on the deck above, the smell of new paint, the lapping of the waves on the side of the ship, the sunset seen through my porthole, and Elman practising Bach's Chaconne."

The quote highlights the fact that the most lavish suites often made the least successful cabins, simply because the designers had insulated the inhabitants from the ocean. Many third class passengers, in cabins which featured nothing more ornate than steel ceilings, exposed pipes, simple bunks and portholes, were continuously reminded that they were on board a ship — and found the experience exciting and unique. However, the same class of passengers did yearn for the luxuries of the first class public rooms, and one of the highlights of any voyage was the attempt at getting in to the first class section of the ship for a look around. Apparently, lounge stewards on the Berengaria always knew that when the chairs all became full, then there had been a massive infiltration from the lower reaches of the ship. The story goes that, on the same ship, the largest ever single invasion of first class occurred on a certain fourth of July, when five hundred tourist class passengers, fired with patriotism, marched defiantly into the first class lounge.

In the years between the wars, competition for Atlantic travel was becoming intense, and once again, Cunard began planning for new ships. The drawing boards were cleared for the design of two new superliners that would become the best-loved merchant ships of all time, and would each carry a royal title.

***Cunard magazine of Summer 1923, when competition for Atlantic passengers was becoming intense (Author photo of Cobwebs collection)***

# II When the Money ran out

In December 1930, the keel was laid on the Clyde for a new 80,000 ton ocean liner – Cunard had plans for a new weekly service carrying up to 2,000 passengers, but suddenly the depression hit.

Six years after the decision was made to plan hull number 534, the directors of Cunard met once again. The hull had cost £1½ million already, and Cunard just couldn't find the rest of the cash needed to get the ship as far as the launching stage, let alone even begin to address the problem of raising another three million for the fitting-out.

It was a hard decision to make, but after Cunard had explored every possible avenue, they were forced to discontinue work on their new ship. Consequently, on Friday December 11, 1931, a notice appeared at John Brown's yard, which told the 3,500 workers that they had to go home. For them, along with almost 10,000 other craftsmen from allied subcontract trades, 1931 was going to end with a very bleak Christmas indeed.

The ship itself had the appearance of a huge skeleton above the Clyde, and its appearance made the men become depressed and nervous. Their meagre savings were soon gone, and rent still had to be paid. In addition, many had wives and children to support. Things were getting so bad that, by 1932, there were petitions at the Local Education Committee pleading for extra food for the children of the unemployed workers. Apparently, many were trying to maintain an existence on half a slice of bread, and, if they were very lucky, a drink of tea. Reports stated that dinner was often nothing more than a penny bone with a few lentils plus vegetables for the better off. This was leading to obvious signs of undernourishment that the worried parents were powerless to resolve.

Cunard, meanwhile was severely in debt, and every remaining employee of the company was forced to take a reduction in salary. This was calculated to save one and three-quarter million pounds in twelve months. Cunard were one of many shipping companies in the same situation: the White Star Line had to cancel their new ship even before work had begun on it. The plight of these once-powerful firms became headline news, and one newspaper, *The Daily Telegraph*, maintained that hull 534 should receive assistance from public funds, suggesting that National pride could be restored if the ship was eventually built.

Perhaps the newspapers influenced the government's decision, or maybe the sentiments printed were something that they secretly had agreed with anyway. At any rate, in October 1932, nearly a whole year after the suspension of work, Neville Chamberlain, who was then the Chancellor of the Exchequer, called a meeting to examine the British steamship companies more closely. A detailed report was requested, and duly submitted by the end of the year. After some deliberation, it was eventually decided that Cunard would be lent money on very favourable terms to allow for the completion of hull 534, and also for the proposed construction of a sister ship (later to become Queen Elizabeth). However, there was a condition that Chamberlain insisted should be met. It was that Cunard must merge with White Star. In the economic climate prevailing at the time, neither were in a position to argue, as well they might well have done several years earlier. And so, buoyed up by a capital injection of £9½ million, Cunard White Star Ltd came into being.

Cunard were the principal shareholders, with sixty-two per cent of the new company. The government money was split three ways, £3 million to complete 534, £1½ million of working capital, and £5 million for a sister ship. The Labour Party fiercely denounced this generous hand-out to a private company, and even some Conservatives voiced their disapproval. However, the Clydeside workers were pleased with the decision, as the re-start would mean work again. This point was a major force in Parliament sanctioning the deal. The stoppage had affected not just the Clyde, but the whole country. Now numerous allied trades were provided with much-needed work. English foundries were able to build huge castings and bearings. Potters began labouring at their wheels to produce 200,000 pieces of crockery, and Sheffield got started on the 100,000 pieces of cutlery required for the ship. An order was given to a Liverpool firm worth £10,000 to supply the glass and a Millwall foundry was to handle the contract for the propellers. In addition, curtain, anchor chains, electric lights, bell pushes and carpets were ordered. The Government's decision had meant that Clydebank's community could rest easy with the prospect of a long term of employment. But above all that, national pride was restored, and once again, Britain would command the Atlantic with the best liner in the world. And so it went that the postman delivered the following letters around Glasgow at the end of March 1934. "Please report to Messrs. John Brown and Co Ltd, Clydebank on Tuesday April 3rd at 7.40 am ready to start work. Please hand the enclosed introduction card to employer."

On the appointed day, the workers were accompanied to their stations by pipers, and were soon busy removing the 130 tons of rust that had formed all over the steel skeleton. Two years and four months had passed, but now at last the world's greatest ship was going to be built.

The whole project was designed to be Big, and as the ship now progressed, the public were continuously enthralled by the media's comparisons. Artist's impressions were published with the huge vessel beside the Eiffel Tower, or the Empire State Building. There was even one drawing of the ship lying across Central London, her bows in Whitehall, and her stern in St Martin's Lane. The excitement amongst the general public grew, and what amazed most people at the time, bearing in mind that the country was in a deep depression, was the cost of the ship — £5 million! In the Thirties, this was an enormous sum. In addition, the ship was to be the first liner over 1,000 feet long, although, as it turned out, the French were first past this mark, when their Normandie pre-dated the Mary due to the stoppages.

On launching, the hull weighed in at 35,500 tons, with the rudder alone weighing 180 tons. Some of the steel plates that made up the hull and decks were up to 30 feet long and over 3 tons each. Straightforward tasks on smaller vessels, such as painting the hull, required 70,000 gallons on the Mary! There were two thousand portholes, and these, together with the other larger windows on the ship apparently required two and a half thousand square feet of thick toughened glass. The ship's whistles could be heard ten miles away and were said to be a note two octaves below middle A. The four propellers, each having four blades, cost £7,000 each, and were manufactured from 50 ton "Turbiston" castings, weighing about 35 tons each. The heaviest propellers ever previously manufactured had been 25 tons, so this was yet another first.

Turbines were the obvious choice for the ship, and quadruple expansion, reduced geared ones were used, with each having 257,000 blades — every single one set by hand. These turbines developed 50,000 horsepower and turned at 3,000 rpm. The speed was reduced down at the propellers themselves to 200 rpm by utilising a fourteen foot diameter reduction gear. Steam was provided by twenty-four Yarrow type water tube boilers, fuelled from oil tanks that held 75,000 gallons. In addition to the high pressure steam, low pressure was available for the kitchens and the heating system, by three double ended "Scotch" boilers. But steam couldn't power everything, and electricity was required to light thirty thousand bulbs, power twenty-two lifts, five hundred and ninety six clocks and numerous other luxury appliances. This was obtained from seven turbo-generator sets that produced 10,000 kilowatts along a total of four thousand miles of electric wiring.

All this and more gave the 776 cabin (first class), 784 tourist (second class) and 579 third class passengers the comfort that they had been primed to expect, assisted by 1,101 officers and crew. Although for some members of the aristocratic public, it was the sheer size of the ship that attracted them and enticed them to become paying customers, for most it was primarily the interior decor. The completed ship set many future trends. Fifty types of wood were used in the construction, some for the first time, having been imported from as far afield as Africa, Asia and America. These included four types of ash, six of mahogany, and four of oak. There were also more exotic ones such as zebrano, thuya and makore.

The story of how the Queen Mary got her name is an interesting one, if it is to be believed. Apparently, Lord Roydon, one of the directors at Cunard, was a personal friend of George V, and so he was detailed to ask for Royal permission to name the ship Victoria (the prefix "ia" was traditional with the company). The King was supposed to have just potted a grouse when Lord Roydon asked: "Would His Majesty consent to the great liner being named after the most illustrious and remarkable woman who has ever been Queen of England?"

"That is the greatest compliment that has ever been made to me or my wife!" replied the King. "I will ask her permission when I get home!" So the ship became, mistakenly, Queen Mary.

The launch itself was carried out in driving rain on September 30, 1934. However, the weather couldn't keep the reputed 200,000 spectators away. Many watched from specially constructed stands, for which they had paid fifteen shillings each to stand on. A large sum for a meagre one hundred seconds of excitement as the metal hull roared into the waters of the Clyde. Chains whipped up, and a flame spurted over the greased way, then the anonymous hull 534 had become the Queen Mary and was riding high in the rain-splattered water. King George V made the following statement: "Today we come to the happy task of sending on her way, the stateliest ship now in being. For three years her unaccomplished hull has lain in silence on the stocks. We know full well what misery a silent dockyard may spread amongst a seaport, and with what courage that misery is endured. During those years when work upon her was suspended, we grieved for what that suspension meant to thousands of our people. We rejoice that, with the help of my Government, it has been possible to lift that cloud and to complete the ship. Now, with the hope of better trade on both sides of the Atlantic, let us look forward to her playing a great part in the revival of international commerce. It has been the Nation's will that she should be completed, and today we can send her forth, no longer a number on the books, but a ship with a name in the world, alive with beauty, energy and strength."

The ship was afloat, and the financial problems were a thing of the past, but the fitting-out of the ship proved to be another obstacle to surmount. Within weeks of the commencement of work, Cunard were having second thoughts about their commissions. The company directors were keen to ensure that the Queen Mary didn't end up looking like the stately homes that the line's other vessels had become in the fitting-out basin, so they ordered a more modern approach, but when they saw the results, they were convinced that they had made a grave error of judgement. For example, Sir Stanley Spencer provided a panel which showed a group of riveters straining to get a large metal plate in place, and Duncan Grant, who was commissioned to decorate the large lounge, executed a striking painting that art critics felt was innovative; Cunard didn't! Sir Percy Bates of the company, apparently thought that the work would be better off "in the blind school". Consequently, in its place, a large mirror was erected.

However, the finished interior was regarded as a triumph for craftsmanship and style. On climbing the gangway and entering the ship in first class, you found yourself in a foyer on C deck. Through revolving doors, you could catch a glimpse of the main pool, whilst to the left was the main staircase and lifts. If one of these was taken to the sports deck, the passenger emerged into the open air with the water 60 feet below. Above, the bridge projected its wings twelve feet each side. Turning around, the three funnels would dominate the view. On the first and second of these, the whistles were fitted. To port and starboard of this deck you could see rows of large ventilators that were designed to suck air

***The Queen Mary leaves John Brown's shipyard on the Clyde on March 3, 1936, whilst one of the men who built her waves farewell (Cobwebs collection)***

down to the regions below. Just aft of the forward funnel was a large open deck where three full-sized tennis courts were marked out. Beside the midships funnel could be found the entrance to the gallery of the squash-racquets court, and behind that, the pet's home, a space designed for passengers' animal companions, with its own uniformed attendant. Further aft, past the lifeboats at the after end was another open space. All in all, the Queen Mary had a total of two acres of deck.

Down a few steps from the sun deck was yet another open space. This one, at the after end, was set aside for first class passengers. From here, one of the most famous of the public rooms could be entered, the Verandah Grill. This was a light and airy room, 70 foot in length and 29 feet wide, with a large circular bay facing aft and looking out to sea. It was used for special à la carte meals for passengers who did not want to visit the main restaurant; an extra charge was levied for the privilege. In the centre was a small dance floor with raised platforms on either side. There were also large wall surface paintings by Doris Zinkeisen. Another feature was the balustrading in cast engraved glass, illuminated from below. Twenty broad windows provided a panoramic view over the stern. These could be opened to lead out onto the wide deck outside, hence the name Verandah Grill.

Adjoining this room were the kitchens, and moving forward you passed the engineer's and officer's private rooms and ward room. Further forward still was the dome of the saloon which rose through three decks, and near the midships funnel casing was the first class gym, decorated by cartoonist Tim Webster. Further along, you came across the squash racquets court, with the gallery for

***One of the most famous public rooms, the verandah grill (Cobwebs collection)***

spectators, mentioned earlier, above. At the end of this deck there were staterooms, and the curved forward end housed the offices of various officials.

Down below, on the promenade deck, was the observation lounge and cocktail bar. On this deck were situated the majority of the main public rooms. The hall into which staircases and lifts descended also had shops within it, and was given the nickname Piccadilly Circus. The observation lounge itself provided a view out across the bows over the fo'c'sle below. This room was some 70 feet wide and over 12 feet high, with a railed observation platform, with ornamental balustrading, for looking out to sea. The colour scheme here was dictated by the use of maze-birch and bubinga woods in dark shades. Over the bar there was a series of paintings by A.R. Thomson, symbolizing various dances.

Just along the corridor could be found the first class children's playroom. This was 40 feet long by 18 feet wide and 12 feet high. It had large windows to make it bright and airy, and the room was split into three divisions. The first was a general centre section, then there were sections on either side devoted to the differing play requirements of boys and girls. There were also slides and hidden caves and a miniature aquarium with tropical fish, in addition to a cinema which children could control themselves. The main feature of the girls section was a large dolls house. Decoration here included walls painted by George Ramon, depicting comic animals.

Opposite this playroom was the library, where all the books were protected from falling out in rough weather by sliding glass panels. The room was fitted with alcoves, and was 43 feet long by 20 feet wide, and finished in subdued tones of cream and brown, treated in pigskin with an oak burr dado, sycamore rails and an ebonized oak skirting. On the floor was a deep pile brown carpet, and the walls featured ebony plaques by Mary Adshead and Steven Bone. At one end stood the librarian's desk, and laid out on a central table could be found all the latest magazines from both sides of the Atlantic, with bookcases providing a choice of 1,700 volumes.

Between the library on the port side, and the drawing room to starboard, you came across a section known as the main hall, with staircases and

***The main hall and shopping centre (Cobwebs collection)***

***There were slides and hidden caves in the playroom (Cobwebs collection)***

lifts at the far end, and several shops nearby. The hall itself measured 111 feet long, and in parts, over 70 feet wide, with walls decorated in figured chestnut. Several notable works of art could be seen there, including a plaster frieze, ivory in tone, by Maurice Lambert, then, looking aft, a marble plaque of the Queen Mary herself. This, set on a panel of walnut burr, was the work of Lady Hilton Young.

The drawing room, across the way had cream painted walls, being some 43 feet in length by 20 feet. At the aft end, over an onyx Doré mantelpiece, hung a decorative panel by Kenneth Shoesmith, and forward was an altar, the altar piece being a painting of the Madonna, executed on a background of gold leaf, whilst on the panels over the doors enclosing the altar could be seen further vividly coloured paintings depicting market scenes with fruit and flowers.

The main lounge, arguably the greatest room on the ship, was reached by leaving the drawing room, passing a small writing room, then entering through a pair of heavy swing doors. This room was lofty, being three decks high. It was 96 feet in length, 70 feet wide, and 22 feet high with walls of a rich golden colour, produced by a combination of maple burr and makore. All the metalwork was finished in dull gold, and the mantelpieces above the electric fires were of golden onyx, whilst above hung paintings by Duncan Grant. The room featured a fully equipped stage that formed the after end. Over this, a series of modelled gilt groups symbolising music, the arts and dancing were placed. These, once again, were designed by Maurice Lambert, and the same artist took responsibility for the ornaments in metal over the forward and aft entrance doors. At the forward end stood a cinema apparatus, and at certain times during the voyage, the room became a 400 seat cinema. By day, the room was bright, having 32 large windows, each being 13 feet high, whilst at night the mood was set by clever concealed lighting.

Leaving the lounge by the after end swing doors, and then through the port doors, you would have found yourself in the Long Gallery. This stretched for 118 feet, and formed a convenient meeting place, as the ballroom was situated at one end, and the lounge at the other. There were two of these galleries: one on the port, and one on the starboard side. Light at night here was subdued, being provided by concealed cornice fittings supplemented by four large and four small illuminated pylons. By day, the Long Gallery featured 22 windows which looked over the promenade deck. The Starboard Gallery, on the other side of the ship, was only about half as long and decorated in grained wood, and on its starboard side, where a casing hid the central funnel uptake, there hung large mural carvings by John Skeaping. Over the doors at either end were electric clocks, and over the fireplaces, two flower studies by Cedric Morris. The room was designed to be used at night as a ladies informal smoking room and lounge, in conjunction with the ballroom that it adjoined. The ballroom itself featured a parquet dance floor just over thirty feet square, and the room itself was 35 feet long by 50 feet wide. On the starboard side, there was a raised platform, with tables and chairs. The colour scheme was predominantly gold, and mirrors were used extensively to give a feeling of open space.

From the ballroom, it was just a few steps to the first class smoking room. This was another lofty area, two decks high, and furnished in the oak and leather of a typical English country club. Alcoves were provided to add character, and in winter, a real coal fire could be lit in the old fashioned dog-grate — the only coal fireplace on the whole ship. The lighting was subdued, and the English brown-oak walls were enhanced by paintings by Edward Wadsworth, whilst higher up, a series of carvings represented playing cards.

Walking outside and heading aft were the tourist quarters, and along this deck, a long vista of

***A long vista of sheltered promenades (Cobwebs collection)***

***The tourist lounge (Cobwebs collection)***

sheltered promenades extended forward to the end of the superstructure to a length of 750 feet. Continuing was the smoking room, decorated in brown and orange, and measuring 42 feet by 70 feet. The floor featured something known as "ruboleum", which was black, sienna and cream, and produced the effect of different coloured planks. Another feature was the settees, placed into alcoves created by screens and providing seating for 106 passengers, whilst over the fireplace was a large marine painting by Charles Pears.

If you made your way downstairs, you would have come to the main deck and be in an area known as the tourist entrance. Just aft of this was the principal tourist lounge. This 16 foot high, 80 foot long and 70 foot wide room had a central dance floor, 33 by 28 feet. At the after end was a stage, and, like the first class lounge, this could be turned into a cinema holding 338 people. The decoration featured coloured hides, with decorative motifs symbolising music, life and dancing.

If you were to turn around and re-pass the tourist entrance and stairs, you would have arrived at the tourist library and writing room. This measured 22 feet long, by 10 feet wide and held 1,400 books. At the end of the library an altar was built, illuminated by subdued lighting and embellished by a painting by Kenneth Shoesmith. The walls were decorated in golden ash and bird's eye maple, with inlaid metalwork in silver bronze. On the starboard side of these rooms could be found the tourist cocktail bar, where glass was the chief decorative effect, and next door to this was the playroom, where boys had railways, forts, soldiers and mechanical monkeys, and girls had a doll's house, with both enjoying a Noah's ark.

Moving through a barrier, which would normally have been locked, brought you to the first class quarters. Right along the ship to the forward end were the private suites and staterooms. Each being individually designed and built using woods ranging from pear tree to cherry. These rooms were single and two berth, and passengers could regulate the temperature and ventilation. In addition, most had en suite facilities, with many bathrooms being lined with synthetic marble. The fare in first class for the round trip to New York and back was £102 off season, and £107 5s in the summer, whilst one way

***There was an altar at one end of the tourist library (Cobwebs collection)***

***Third class garden lounge (Cobwebs collection)***

fares ranged from £53 15s off season, to £56 10s in the summer.

At the forward end of the main deck, we would pass from the sleeping quarters for the first class passengers, to the third class Garden Lounge. Even this was very well-appointed, and better than first class on many ships of the era. Wide windows looked out across the bows, and there were big staircases, comfortable furniture and many plants and flowers.

On the deck below, designated A, was another third class area — the smoking room. This was situated at the extreme forward end of the deck, and also had windows looking out over the bows. Decoration here was in two shades of oak. From this room it was only a short walk to the staircase, complete with shops and lifts, where the purser's office and safe deposit was situated.

Walking aft along veneered corridors of light golden colour, many staterooms would be passed: Amidships were the private suites consisting of sitting room, bedroom, bathroom and toilet, all decorated in different harmonising colour schemes. At the extreme aft end of this deck was another tourist lounge, smaller than the one on the deck above, but still including a bar and ample dance floor. It had sound equipment installed to allow passengers to hear the live dance band relayed from the ballroom, or listen to the ship's orchestra playing in the lounge.

A small flight of stairs led down onto B deck, which was devoted chiefly to private staterooms. The accommodation for the tourist passenger extended through five decks from A to E. Even in these rooms, hot and cold running water was available, with bathrooms and lavatories nearby, whereas in the higher-priced cabins of tourist class, these refinements were included in the cabin itself. Off season fares for a round trip were advertised at £52 10s.

At the fore end of B deck were two rooms, the third class lounge and cinema. Each of these measured over 60 feet in length and was 30 feet wide, with the same entrance serving both rooms. The wall panelling was in cherry wood, with bronze decorations, and one part of the lounge formed a library, whilst the cinema had a raised stage and could, like first and tourist class rooms, be set-up for cine film performances. Next to this was the third class children's playroom, and next to that, the scroll room or synagogue. Moving lower into the ship, onto C deck, we would have been faced with some very popular rooms — the restaurants. On this dining deck were situated the eating places for all three travelling classes, and a rumoured ten thousand meals were served on this deck each day, with the catering personnel accounting for some 800 of the total ship's company.

The tourist dining room was decorated in a light shade of mahogany, and featured a floor space of 90 feet by over 100 feet. Amidships was the first class restaurant, which extended across the full width of the ship, 118 feet, and was some 160 feet in length. It's height passed through three decks, and it was said that the Britannia, the first Cunarder, could easily fit into the confines of this room, which seated 815 people. The walls were veneered in mellow peroba wood, relieved by silver bronzed metalwork. On one wall, a decorative map by Macdonald Gill showed the Queen Mary moving on her course across the Atlantic, so that at any time, a glance revealed the position of the ship. There were also Bainbridge Copnall carvings showing shipping through the ages, and, at the after end, Philip Connard had a large painting symbolizing various forms of travel. Heavy cast bronze doors were used too, designed by Walter Gilbert. Lighting was courtesy of concealed cornice bulbs in cut-glass fittings, fixed onto the large structural columns. All furnishing was finished in sycamore, and the coverings of the chairs were rose pink.

Aft of the restaurant you would come to the kitchens, where over 100 cooks under a chief chef were employed. Moving further aft, was the tourist dining saloon, with seating capacity for just over 400 people, stretching the whole width of the ship. This room measured 78 feet by 118 feet. The decoration featured maple built in courses of different colours. Daylight entered through windows four feet high, and at night by floodlit inner windows which gave an illusion of sunlight. The room also contained a number of sandblasted decorative glass panels, symbolical of fruits of the earth.

Leaving this deck, and moving further down into the ship onto D deck, were more tourist cabins, and on the port side, the storage rooms and refrigerated space of 60,000 cubic feet. Also on this deck were the ship's wine cellars, where 10,000 wines, 40,000 bottles of beer, and 60,000 bottles of mineral waters were often stored. Forward on D deck was the hospital, with its male and female wards, dispensary and operating theatre. Close to this was the print shop which handled all the notices, menus and ship's newspaper. Further forward again was situated the first class swimming pool. This had cream tiling, a wide balcony and a ceiling of glass. The pool itself was 22 feet wide, by 35 feet long, and provided with a chute and a deep and shallow end. From the pool balcony, the Turkish bath could be reached, together with the massage rooms.

The third class staterooms were on E deck, and a round trip in this class would have cost at least £33 10s. Even further down into the bowels, on F deck, was another popular area, the tourist swimming pool. This was the first covered-in pool for this class of passenger ever built into a ship. It was decorated with blue tiles, and the pool itself measured 33 feet by 21 feet. Adjoining this could be found a fully-equipped tourist gymnasium.

Artistic masterpieces weren't all restricted to the upper echelons, and a favourite hung in the tourist class smoking room. It was by Charles Pears and depicted a view of the old Mauretania travelling under the Forth Bridge for the last time, heading for the Rosyth breakers yard. The ship was painted white with golden rust streaking down her hull. Her masts were sliced off to allow the passage under the bridge. A sad end to an earlier Atlantic favourite.

A total of thirty-six artists were invited to submit works. There were complaints from some quarters, who felt that the finished effect was a rather disjointed hotch-potch of styles as opposed to a complete unified whole that had marked the earlier Cunarders. Apparently, some considered that the plastic laminates paired up with woods and strip lighting had the appearance of Leicester Square, London, but Cunard were quick to point out that millions of people visited that attraction, and enjoyed it!

In Southampton, which was to become the Queen Mary's home port, preparations had been under way for years, and there had been numerous business arguments before a satisfactory arrangement had eventually been agreed. At one stage, it looked as if Southampton wouldn't become

***The first class restaurant (Cobwebs collection)***

***The third class staterooms were on E deck (Cobwebs collection)***

the new liner's home at all, due to the fact that the dock's owners, the Southern Railway Company, under Sir Herbert Walker, were very reluctant to build the necessary £1.85 million dry dock to house the ship. They were concerned that it would end up being used just twice a year, and consequently provide no more than approximately £10,000 per annum in revenue. The negotiations became quite protracted, and looked like dragging on for some time until Sir Percy Bates of Cunard is reputed to have delivered an ultimatum of "no dock, no ship". He maintained that Liverpool could easily become the home port, and that Cunard were quite capable of building their own dock in a suitable southern port. This seemed to have the desired effect, and the new dock was duly constructed. It was 1,200 feet long, and was eventually opened on July 26, 1933 by the King and Queen who sailed in on their Royal Yacht, "Victoria and Albert".

The Queen Mary finally anchored off Cowes in late spring 1936. Three quarters of a million people had gathered on the shorelines to watch her ease her way through the Solent accompanied by countless small boats. By evening, she was out of the water once more, in dry dock. Her hull was cleaned and repainted, and the remaining launch fittings removed. During this time, thousands of people were offered tours of the ship at one shilling each.

On April 8, the new liner was floated out of the dock and moored opposite another famous Cunarder, the Aquitania. There she lay until the 15th, when she left for speed trials off the island of Arran. At the time, and prematurely as it turned out, the ship was described as "perfect with vibrationless qualities".

***The Queen Mary finally anchored off Cowes in late spring 1936 (Author photo of Cobwebs collection)***

***The new Queen in the equally new dry dock in Southampton that caused all the fuss (Cobwebs collection)***

QUEEN MARY
LIVERPOOL

***The Queen Mary sails from Southampton on her maiden voyage amidst cheering crowds (Cobwebs collection)***

The trials did accurately illustrate the Mary's potential speed which would be her saviour in the following war years, and speeds of over 32.84 knots were claimed during tests. Following these trials, the liner returned once again to Southampton, and was officially handed over to Cunard White Star on May 12. Two days later, there was a special short cruise for representatives of the builders, outfitters and contractors, then, for the next three days, the liner was again opened to the public, with complete tours of the ship (not just the decks this time) costing five shillings. All proceeds were donated to seaman's charities, with fifteen thousand people taking advantage of the tours. After the visitors had left, the King and his mother, Queen Alexandra, toured the vessel, and, on leaving, presented signed portraits of themselves. The Queen Mother's standard was then fixed to the bulkhead on the main staircase.

On May 27, 1936, the Queen Mary was complete to Cunard's satisfaction, and she sailed on her maiden voyage. Once again, the shorelines near Southampton were packed with crowds. On board, together with the passengers and crew, was Henry Hall and the Queen Mary Orchestra. He was required to play fourteen live concerts from the ship which were broadcast to radio listeners direct by the BBC. The maiden voyage was later described as a "long festival" and a "joyful cruise experience" with the champagne flowing freely for everyone including the crew. Passengers were given a commemorative medallion of the voyage, and the ladies were treated to a silver-plate powder compact which bore an enamelled portrait of the ship. During the crossing, a wreath was laid in the water at the spot where the White Star liner Titanic had so tragically gone down after striking an iceberg in 1912.

The arrival in New York proved to be among the most spectacular in the port's maritime history, and many craft, both on the sea and in the air, greeted the great new liner as she steamed in. A plane flew over the ship and unleashed a rain of flowers, while cheering crowds almost drowned out the brass bands which played on the quayside. In New York docks, a £2 million pier had been built to house the new Cunarder, and after berthing at this,

***The arrival in New York proved to be among the most spectacular in the port's maritime history (Wrather Port Properties photo)***

the celebrations continued, and it was estimated that around 30,000 visitors boarded the ship and took at least one souvenir each when they eventually left.

Underneath the excitement, Cunard were in a dilemma; the pride of Britain's marine engineering was absolutely terrible at sea, a fact that had somehow passed unnoticed during the earlier trials. She rolled desperately from side to side, and rattled and vibrated at the stern. The ship had a worrying tendency to roll, then hold for a moment or so, and then continue the roll as if she was about to capsize. Finally, after another few very anxious moments, she would steady herself and repeat the movement on the other side. This was a major problem that was difficult to solve, and would unfortunately remain with the ship for the first twenty years of her career. It was this, along with the awful vibrations, that forced Cunard to withdraw the ship from service after a few months for what they claimed were "routine overhauls". The resultant work was carried out very furtively, and amounted to an enormous strip-down which involved the total removal of the great lounge, the smoking room, and most of the luxurious staterooms. This could hardly be classed as routine, and neither could the 18 inch circumference, steel stanchions that were bolted across the top of the wobbly liner either! Cunard had to suffer in embarrassed silence over this, as all the way along the hull were fixed twelve by fourteen inch channel beams that intermeshed with the thick steel crossbeams. This really was an admission of construction failure which, thankfully, was ignored by the press who knew what was occurring, but elected to maintain silence, feeling that it would damage the rising public pride.

Other minor faults hushed up at the time included problems with smut and grit blowing down onto the deck from the funnels. The story goes that several passengers were paid handsomely for their silences over this matter, and filters were added as soon as was practical. But that wasn't all, the propellers had been fitted in a blaze of glory, and thousands of admirers had even autographed them when a public inspection was invited before fitting. But now they were a source of more red faces for Cunard White Star, and were taken off and sold quietly for scrap after just a few voyages, to be replaced by a brand new, completely redesigned set to minimize the vibrations. Furthermore, there were problems with the furniture and fittings. Cunard were so convinced that the liner would be completely stable in mid-ocean, that they didn't bother to bolt anything down, or provide adequate stowage for breakables. Because of this false confidence, the potters back in England found themselves working extra shifts to keep up with the demand for new items destined for the ship. As quickly as the rapid replacements were delivered, they were broken again.

Unfortunately, it wasn't simply the rigours of

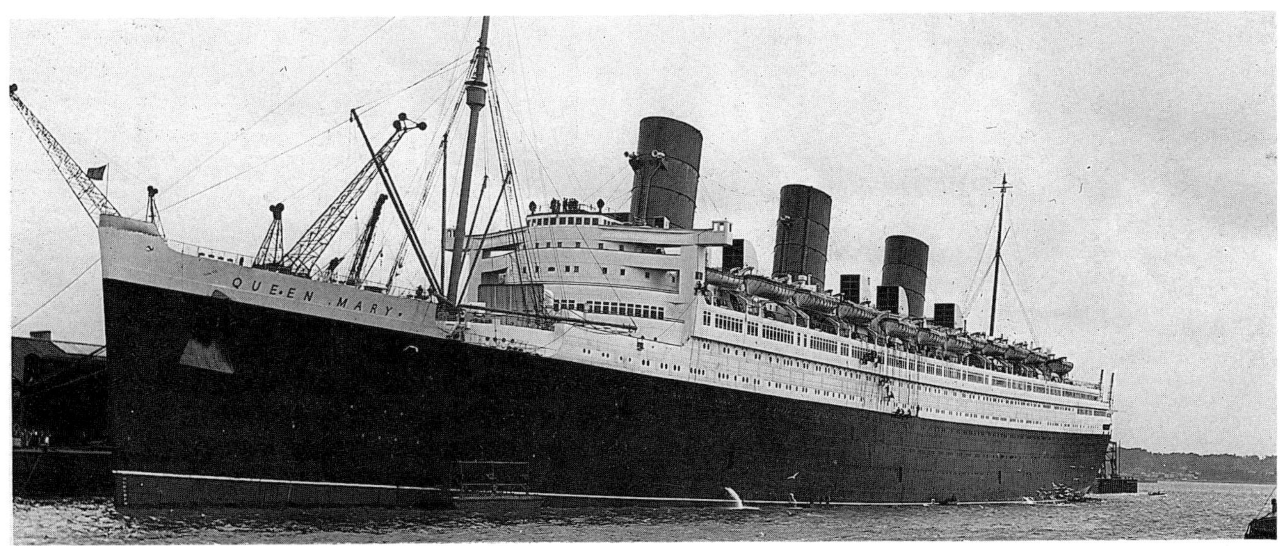


***In the first year, Cunard were offering trips on hire-purchase (Cobwebs collection)***

the ocean that were causing problems. Much of the damage sustained to the interior of the ship on the first few voyages was caused by human hands hunting for prized souvenirs to take home and display. In New York, traders were selling mementos of the ship, but most passengers didn't buy because they all had their own sections of the real thing, such as ashtrays, tea services, cutlery, brass notices, nameplates, condiments and even paintings. However, the majority of Britain's general public knew nothing of all this. For them, the only disappointment was that the ship hadn't captured the coveted Blue Riband on her maiden voyage. There was great secret rivalry at the time between the Queen Mary and the Normandie, even though Cunard wouldn't actually admit to it. Instead, they maintained that they weren't interested in racing. In public, the Captain would often excuse any excess speed by putting it down to "operational requirements", such as ensuring that the ship was making necessary speed to catch the tides at Cherbourg or Southampton. However, Geoffrey Marr, who became commodore of the line years later called this mere fiction, and the timetable was subtly altered so that the ship could do crossings of over 30 knots, even though the normal service speed was 28.5.

In reality, both the Mary and the Normandie were similar in many ways; their tonnages were approximately equal, and they were comparable in length, with the Normandie being slightly longer. However, the French ship had clipper bows and a thirty-eight foot overhang at the stern. When these "useless" areas were subtracted, then the Queen Mary was the longer vessel. The competition between the two giants forced Cunard to give good deals to passengers. In the first year, the company were offering trips on hire-purchase, with twenty five per cent down, and a year to pay off the balance.

Some of the press comments of the period are interesting to look back on, especially one from the *New York Herald Tribune*, which read "Ease: takes the sea without vibration or uncomfortable roll", obviously the reporter hadn't been on board! Or the one that said, "You'll find yourself secretly grateful that there are no screaming colours." Yet there undoubtedly were. Another classic was the comment that the ship was "as sweet as the English air could make her," even though she had been constructed entirely in Scotland. Some were nearer the mark though, and the *New Yorker*'s comment that "the Queen Mary is just about the most beautiful ship afloat," and *The New York Times*'s "A new peak in luxury at sea," were much more accurate.

The Blue Riband was soon in Cunard's hands, when, in August 1936, the Queen Mary made the very first Atlantic crossing in under four days. Sir Peter Bates explained, in characteristic Cunard style, why they'd done it: "While we have let out the Queen Mary during this voyage, we had an object in what we were doing. We are at the moment engaged in consideration of the details of the Queen Mary's sister ship. To help us to a proper consideration of the details of the machinery and the propellers, the round voyage such as the Queen Mary has run this last fortnight will be of great assistance.

Accordingly, before the ship started on the last voyage I took counsel with the builders and our own technical experts, and the figures which we have obtained as a result of this voyage will be of the greatest assistance in considering Hull number 552 in the next few weeks."

# III
# Lessons Learned

A Cunard spy masquerading as a grocer may have helped the Queen Elizabeth to become the "ultimate ship" that she was dubbed at the time. Apparently, he travelled on the Normandie and peppered the crew about shaft horsepower, reduction geared turbines and boiler pressures. The crew of the great French ship may have thought that he was planning some massive sort of baking oven.

Whether or not his information was valuable, on December 6, 1938, the keel was laid in John Brown's shipyard on the Clyde for another great Cunard liner, initially to be known as Hull 552. The building process begins with a thousand foot stretch of earth sloping into the waters of the Clyde, flanked on either side by large cranes. A gang of men handle large pitch pine blocks, building them lengthwise and crosswise into pyramids. These blocks finally lay in a dead straight line down the centre of the berth to the river, placed to support the weight of the ship that will be built above them. The slope of about nine-sixteenths of an inch to the foot down to the water has to be even and exact, and for Hull 552, it was necessary to strengthen the ground of the building berth further by driving in timber.

Whilst all this is going on, inside the Clydebank drawing offices, many detailed plans are being finalized. From the drawing office, the plans go to the mould loft. "Lofting" as it is termed, is one of the most skilled jobs in the yard. The loft itself is an enormous shed whose only apparatus, apart from the line of carpenter's benches along one wall, is a vast, entirely bare, black-painted floor. On this is drawn a mass of white chalk curves and parallels which reveal the shape of various parts of the ship's hull, and also of every plate that will go to make it. These lines are marked out in their actual size from detailed plans prepared in the drawing office.

The next stage takes place in the forges and plating sheds. The smithy's iron floor is punched through with lots of holes which assist in the shaping of the steel bars whose curves have previously been patterned in the mould loft, but it is in the plating sheds that the actual hull skeleton really begins to take shape. There, rows of large machines, attended by craftsmen, cut, stamp and shear the plates and frames: Into the plating sheds come rough-cut plates and bars of only approximate size. Out must go precise, perfect fitting components that can be swung directly into place on the hull by cranes, ready for the riveters.

The keel is built from large 'V' and 'U' frames, which have plates riveted to them. In this fashion, the ship's skin is gradually built up whilst more riveters and platers begin fitting the beams and laying the decks. The original pyramids of keel blocks are joined by a forest of wooden props which support the weight of 552 that was to measure 1,031 feet. On paper, the job sounds straightforward: in reality it is far from it!

As work progressed in the late thirties, it looked

certain that, for the first time in history, a British express service would soon be maintained between Southampton and New York, using just two liners. The long hoped for and carefully planned schedule of weekly crossings from both sides of the Atlantic was the principal reason that each of the ships was to be so large. Sir Percy Bates of Cunard explained: "The speed is dictated by the time necessary to perform the journey at all seasons of the year, and the size is dictated by the necessity to make money to pay for the speed. To go beyond these conditions would be extravagant; to fall below them would be incompetent."

Hull 552 was started amongst widespread optimism. Britain was free of the depression, the Queen Mary was on the verge of profit, and Cunard were certain that their new ship would follow in her sister's successful footsteps. The only possible threat, as far as the line were aware, was from the Normandie. However the Second World War made this irrelevant. Whilst undergoing conversion work for the American Navy, the Normandie caught fire and capsized at her pier. Although later salvaged, it was obvious that the ship could never be returned to her former quality, and so she was subsequently broken up.

Lessons had been learned from the Queen Mary, and faults that had become apparent on the earlier ship were avoided on Hull 552. In addition this time around, Cunard were financially secure, with the £5 million government budget for the new ship at their disposal. One of the first improvements was a significant one for the passengers, of the era, and it was a careful revision of proposed deck allocation. On board the Queen Mary, there had been criticisms raised from the first class passengers, who disliked the fact that they were overlooked by the tourist class travellers who could peer down on them strolling on the boat deck from their allocated deck behind the bridge. At the time, class segregation on ships was very much in evidence, and this was considered a serious oversight by Cunard. This, coupled with the fact that 552 was to have just two funnels, and hence more deck space, ensured that this problem was not repeated. The ship's forward funnel was to be over seventy feet above the sun deck, and measured, in cross-section, 44 feet by 30, large enough to allow the passage of three big locomotives of the era to pass through abreast. Another distinguishing feature about the ship's funnel design in comparison to the Queen Mary's, was that all external guys and stays were dispensed with, and the whistle steampipes and other fittings were concealed inside. Boiler-room and other ventilators were also absent, replaced by more modern air intakes. In addition, the upper decks were terraced towards the stern to provide even more deck space, and offer a much more graceful overall appearance.

Many advanced techniques were pioneered with Hull 552, one being the double bottom, two hull skins separated by about six feet. The shell itself was divided up by fifteen watertight bulkheads, and it was stated at the time that in excess of ten million rivets were used in its construction. Furthermore, technological advances had meant that only twelve instead of twenty-four boilers were required, occupying a deck space some four stories high. The engine room of the Queen Elizabeth, like her sister ship, was to feature geared steam turbines. Steam from her oil burning boilers would be forced at high pressure on to the blades of the turbine rotors, and each rotor would spin at high speed to drive the shaft which would be geared down before the drive communicated with the propeller shafts themselves. The oil fuel would be carried in side bunkers near the boiler-rooms, and in double-bottomed tanks amidships. The main machinery arrangement was planned as follows: number one boiler-room, number two boiler-room, water softening and air conditioning plants, turbo generator rooms, number three boiler-room, number four boiler-room, forward engine-room, and aft engine-room.

Steam would be provided by 12 large Yarrow-type water tube boilers provided with superheaters and large pre-heaters. Twelve electrically driven Howden fan units would supply air to the boilers for combustion with a working pressure of 425lb. per square inch, and a steam temperature of 750 degrees F. The closed stokehold system, whereby air would be forced into the boiler-room and thence through the pre-heaters to the furnaces, was used instead of the closed trunk system of forced draught, and the ship's boilers would be equipped for oil-fired burning on the Wallsend-Howden system. Exhaust gases from the boilers of number one and number two boiler-rooms would lead to the forward funnel, and from number three and number four boiler-rooms to the after funnel. The four propelling machinery units would be able to operate independently, with each consisting of a high-pressure, a first intermediate pressure, a second intermediate pressure, and a low pressure turbine and condenser. Each of these turbines would drive a separate pinion engaging with a main gear wheel coupled to the forward end of the appropriate propeller shafting. The weight of the four main gear wheels together would be 320 tons. Reduction to the correct propeller speed would be achieved by the use of single-reduction, double-helical gearing, with teeth of the involute design, giving a total output of 160,000 S.H.P, with each of the four shafts fitted with four-bladed manganese-bronze propellers weighing 32 tons. Each set of machinery would be available for independent use to assist manoeuvring, with astern turbines incorporated in each of the second intermediate pressure and low pressure turbine castings.

Virtually all the auxiliary machinery in the main engine-rooms and boiler-rooms would be operated by electricity, and so two separate electric power stations that would provide for the ship's entire electrical requirements, were planned for either side of a centre-line watertight bulkhead between number two and number three boiler-rooms. Each power station would consist of two main generator units which, although independent of each other, could be connected so that in the event of a breakdown in one of them, a complete service throughout the ship would be available from the other. Further back-up was going to be available from two 75 kw emergency generators, driven by oil engines.

Each of the ship's generators were to consist of two dynamos of 1,100 kilowatts capacity, driven in tandem by a steam turbine revolving at 4,500 revolutions per minute. This would be geared down at the dynamos to a speed of 600 revs., and when all four generators were in operation, the total output power would be 8,000 kilowatts. However, it was reasoned that full power would rarely be required, and therefore, one generator could normally remain idle for routine maintenance purposes.

However, at launching, the ship was still no more than a vast steel shell. The most pressing problem at that time was not the engines, but the transferring of the weight of the hull, which had reached 30,000 tons, from the blocks on which her keel rested and the shores which supported her sides, to the launching ways. The ship had to be lifted on wedges clear of her original supports, then ground ways laid on either side, looking like a pair of outsize railway tracks. On these ground ways, the sliding ways rested, and between these two sets of ways, hundredweights of melted grease and tallow was poured. The space between the ship and the sliding ways was made up with baulks of timber over the flat portions, whilst at the finer points of the ship, forward and aft, closely spaced vertical timbers were fitted to form cradles. Between the sliding ways, wedges were inserted, and by driving on these wedges, some of the weight of the ship could be transferred to the sliding ways themselves. This done, the only thing that prevented the ship from slipping away was a small number of sturdy wedges driven between the two sets of ways.

By the time the ship had been thus prepared, the threat of war was upon the country, and on September 27, 1938, Queen Elizabeth had to perform the ceremony without King George VI, who could not be present because of the mounting problems facing his country. Hull 552 was impatient to be named, and began to move forward a few inches 72 hours before the appointed launch time. When the ceremony did take place, Her Majesty the Queen gave the liner her own name, and a considerable crowd gathered to see the ship enter the River Clyde. Because of the possibility of war, the atmosphere was tense as the Queen made her speech: "The launching of a ship is like the inception of a great human enterprise, an act of faith. We cannot foretell the future, but in preparing for it, we show our trust in Divine Providence. We proclaim our belief that by the grace of God and by man's patience and goodwill, order may yet be brought out of the confusion, and peace out of turmoil. With that hope and prayer in our hearts, we send forth on her mission, this noble ship."

On August 22, 1939, Cunard, still hopeful of peace, announced the maiden voyage, which was planned for April 24, 1940, but this was not to be, and within a few weeks, work had been suspended on the fitting-out of the new Cunarder because of the outbreak of war. There followed urgent conferences with the top executives of the company and the government, and further work was authorised so that the shell could in fact be made seaworthy and moved to a safer location – Hitler's bombs were already a threat.

Following this, in February 1940, a crew of 400

were assembled and the ship was on her way. She duly left the fitting-out basin on the Clyde on the 26th, and there was a small handing-over ceremony. It was the first time ever in maritime history where there had been no prior tests or trials. Following this, Captain Townley set the new Queen off on her maiden voyage down towards Southampton. On the way, he opened his secret orders and found that his actual destination was to be New York. This following excerpt from a British newspaper of Thursday March 7, 1940, sums up the scene: "SECRET OF BRITAIN'S GREATEST LINER IS OUT. QUEEN ELIZABETH SMUGGLED TO U.S. RACES ACROSS ATLANTIC TO DODGE NAZI RAIDERS. Britain's newest liner, the £5,000,000 Queen Elizabeth, was safe in New York harbour last night after a secret dash across the Atlantic. The biggest ship in the world joins her companion liner, the Queen Mary, in security from Nazi raiders. The Queen Elizabeth called the "noblest ship ever launched" was in a fitting out basin in the Clyde from September 27, 1938, when the Queen launched her, until ten days ago. Then she was taken secretly down the Clyde. After that – silence, until it was known last night that the 85,000 ton liner had reached the end of her maiden voyage."

A further, rather colourful, tabloid report of the period provides an important insight into the mood of the nation: "A ghost ship slid between the clouded banks of the Clyde ten days ago. She looked as if she was in mourning, for though she was a passenger liner, she was painted battleship grey. No one was supposed to know her name. That, too, was embedded in grey paint. There were no flags, no bunting, no streamers. There was no one to see her away from the basin where she was born, except the men who built her. They were not sure whether to cheer, for she was stillborn. This liner has been given a Royal launching, and her name was the grandest in shipping. Yet we stood on the bankside watching her go on the slow uncertain voyage to the sea under a haze of anonymity. It was secret; yet the whole of Clydebank knew. The word had gone round the cottages on the river's edge and on the bank were the wives and children of the men that built her. The secret could be hidden from the world, but not from those people. The Queen Elizabeth is the pride of the men who build great ships along the river, and their wives had to see her go, so the Clydebank kept this day to themselves. There was no official party. There were no top hats from London. The workmen had the privileged view from a crane; and stewards and cooks walked the decks. I remember four years ago, watching the Queen Mary pass this way. She was gaudy with new paint, and bunting dripped from her like a feather boa, trailing in the sea. Her name shone in the sun, and the banks of the river were covered like ant hills. Stands were built in the ploughed fields so that all could see her. There was a fairground, with bands and lemonade stands, and the cheering echoed over the hills in great waves. But this great ship, widowed from service by the war, had to take her sailing in silence. The cheer that came from the banks dissolved thinly into the hills behind. There was no echo. All the morning, police launches had gone up and down the channel clearing the traffic. Heavy tugs hovered at the water's edge. Dredgers constantly cleared the grey water – as if that was not enough to tell the Clyde. At one o'clock, a spiral of white smoke rose from two grey funnels that for eighteen months had been an immovable part of the landscape of houses and cranes. She moved like a skyscraper with a swarm of tugs buzzing around her like water beetles. They were the same tugs that had been dressed with flags for the Queen Mary. This time they were in their natural cloak of smoke and dirt. In dead silence they bullied the liner down the twisting, difficult river. Like a grey shadow she moved past fields and houses and the warmth of the countryside. She looked unreal and cumbersome; for a liner needs the open sea to give her beauty the right frame.

The Clydesiders were unhappy about it. They said it was a great pity that this, the loveliest ship afloat, should go away like that – ignobly, unseen. They wanted the ship to be admired. We stood on the bankside picking out the vague lines of the sun decks, the tennis courts and the swimming pool. We could even spot the row of dog kennels around the bottom of the funnels. It will be a long time before an actress's pet dog is locked in one of them.

The tugs dragged her down towards the trap where the river bends sharply and the mud from the fields goes into the river. Four years ago, the Queen Mary "kissed the mud" on each side at this place, as she straddled across the narrow channel. Tugs fretted and pushed and pulled and the ship was free. She passed people standing in their front gardens who could almost have touched her. Then the grey shape disappeared in the mist and smoke, and was round another bend. The people went back to their houses and shut their doors. She left the towns, got pushed into deeper waters. The people on the hillsides went home, and the workmen went back to another job. One day the Queen Elizabeth will be painted with colour. One day she will take her place on the Atlantic."

After the ship's war service, (which is detailed in chapter four) work resumed on the fitting-out of the interior, which was to be styled altogether lighter than the Queen Mary. For example, in the Captain's cabin, the veneer was a shade of light grey, and was explained by means of a special plaque: "The timber used for the lining of this cabin, though botanically known as Ulmus Americanus, or Rock Elm, has the popular designation of Waterloo Elm. It was obtained from the piles driven in 1911 under the original Waterloo Bridge over the River Thames. The change to grey was caused by the bleaching action of tidal waters and discovered when the piles were withdrawn in 1936 to prepare for the new bridge."

The Queen Elizabeth featured many beautiful woods, and there were still unmistakable thirties influenced designs, such as Art Deco motifs over the staircases and artificial fireplaces. The overriding image was one of bleached wood in coffee and cream colours. Cunard felt no desire to break with their age old "gloss and polish" tradition, and whilst the liner was undoubtedly modern for its time, it still clung to many old interior design ideas.

One of the principal works of art on board was a bas relief entitled Oceanides. This was placed at the top of the stairs on the promenade deck square. It was quite risqué, and composed of "the nude figures of a man and a woman in eurythmic attitude." However, for all this, the decor on the Queen Elizabeth was more restrained than on her sister ship. Some felt the ship was already slightly old-fashioned directly after the war because a considerable amount of decorative components were actually completed on shore before the conflict, but not fitted to the ship until seven years

***The promenade square (Cobwebs collection)***

hence. Strangely, as we shall see in a later chapter, most of the crewmen who had the privilege of serving on both ships seemed to favour the Mary, even though she was older. Apparently, they found her an easier ship to work with, and therefore, happier. It was difficult to pinpoint exactly why, but some felt that it was the organised chaos in which the Queen Elizabeth was finally completed that contributed to this fact.

The Queen Elizabeth had fourteen decks, of which four, the sports, sun, boat and promenade were in her superstructure. Of the remaining ten, the upper six were where most of the passenger accommodation was situated and which housed the public rooms. In the days of the Queen Elizabeth, there were three passenger classes, first, cabin and tourist. Tourist accommodation was amidships on D deck, and forward on the four decks above with the capacity for approximately 745 passengers in this section of the ship. There were thirty-five sets of lifts on board to ease travel around the ship, but the staircases were also worthy of note, being enriched with oak veneer panelling.

The tourist dining saloon ran the full width of the ship and seated 400 passengers at tables of two to eight places. On the wall of this room hung a large decorated panel of glass on which was a superimposed clock with a glass dial. Above, on B deck was the tourist lounge, where walnut veneer was used extensively. On one wall stood a full bookcase, and opposite the entrance, one of the many marquetry works – a landscape scene designed by George Ramon.

On A deck there was a tourist smoking room which also ran the width of the ship and was decorated with veneers of pale, straight-grained elm together with marquetry panels. The accommodation here featured deep recessed bays with settees and easy chairs around small round tables, together with a bar at the after end in silver-bronze and cross-banded elm.

There were many rooms for the tourist passenger, of which the Winter Garden on the main deck deserves a mention. It was an airy semi-circular room whose windows overlooked the main deck. At the entrance was a large glass screen which stood in mullions of silver bronze and carried an etched design by Ralph Cowan called "The Birth of Life". The room also featured a display of fresh flowers in jardinieres and bowls below the screen, and round glass columns in the centre of the room.

Special, thoughtful touches had also been added, and the story goes that designers, having reasoned that ladies in evening dress were already sufficiently in competition with their fellow passengers without having to compete with over-colourful decorative scenes, ensured softness and restraint that allowed dresses to look their best. In addition, they apparently searched out a rare earth which, when compounded into glass, cut the yellow of the spectrum, and gave to artificial light, "a radiance which enhances skin tones."

The largest staircase on board was in Cabin Class, aft of D deck, which had 72 of the 720 cabin class passenger staterooms grouped around it, with the remainder living aft and amidships on the four decks above. The staircase featured a dado of elm burr edged with Australian walnut, with a frieze about it of a light vellum tone achieved by bleached Queensbury silky oak. The storm rails and firescreen were green, and niches featured green Poole Pottery vases floodlit from above. At the head of this staircase was a photographic mural of English scenes. However, if passengers were feeling lazy, then there were plenty of lifts carrying abstract designs by Hector Whistler inlaid in aluminium foil.

The cabin class staterooms in colour schemes of either blue, salmon, green or brown, were on A and B decks and all had toilet, mirror and wash basin, with many including a bath and shower, too. The public rooms for this passenger class began with the dining saloon equipped with a series of brilliantly floodlit silver bays, in each of which was a large glass disc etched with flowers. The furniture was in mahogany veneered with coral burr, and on the walls hung two mirrors by Margot Gilbert etched with scenes representing summer and winter carnivals.

Following dinner in cabin class, many passengers adjourned to the lounge on the main deck. This room could hold 200 people easily and had wide, curving windows at one end from which could be seen the whole of the after part of the ship. Pale vellum hung on the walls interspersed with thin bands of silver-bronze. In addition, there were silver surfaces of spun glass, together with two engraved maps showing northern and southern hemispheres. Pale veneers were used on the furniture and the carpeting pattern was of squares which could be rolled back to reveal a parquet floor for dancing.

***The first class restaurant (Cobwebs collection) (Above)***

***The verandah grill, reserved for first class passengers and situated on the sun deck (Cobwebs collection) (Below)***

One deck higher, the first superstructure deck, was the cabin class smoking room, cocktail bar, drawing room and library. The smoking room was classed as one of the most beautiful on the ship with furniture of tan, blue and cream hide which was repeated in the carpet colour. There was also a fireplace surrounded by Maltese marble with three electric fires in the grate. Above this was a panel of nine bas reliefs by Norman Forest highlighting the nine materials used in the construction of the ship, steel, wood, copper, bronze, aluminium, lead, white metal, rubber and glass.

Behind the smoking room could be found the cocktail bar, with double doors connecting the rooms. In here round-the-clock sunlight was produced with the aid of hidden lights and pale yellow spun glass laminated between sheets of clear glass. Behind the bar itself were two Margot Gilbert paintings called "Wine", and "Beer". From the room's windows, the ship's stern was again visible. The nearby library stored 1,200 books, and was close to the drawing room with it's walls hung with flowered silks. This room could be part-enclosed as a chapel for the celebration of Mass, by simply closing folding doors.

With so much catering to be done, it is unsurprising that most of one deck was given over to kitchens. This deck was between B and C, and was termed R deck. More power was fed to these kitchens than supplied to the rest of the ship put together. For ease of serving, the first class restaurant was also situated on this deck, and in the two deck high foyer there was panelling in soft tones of English olive and ash burr. However, the dominating feature of the room was a carving of the Arms of H.M. Queen Elizabeth by Bainbridge Copnall in lime tree wood. There were three more carvings by the same artist hanging on the restaurant walls – a large clock surrounded by lime wood carvings of the zodiac, and two studies, one called "The Fisherman" and the other "The Huntress". This first class restaurant stretched the width of the ship, and measured about 111 feet each way. The square was broken by including a large central portion which divided side aisles, which were in turn divided into bays with sea views. Veneers of London plane tree burr finished in tones of coffee and milk provided the room's dignity, and diners who wanted privacy could book separate rooms leading off from three of the four corners of the restaurant. These were decorated with English elm veneer, willow and brown leather, and white and claret leather. The fourth corner led off to a small secluded cocktail bar.

If the first class passenger preferred, he could dine on the sun deck in the Verandah Grill. This room, like a similar one on the Queen Mary, was designed for dancing and music. It's walls with their veneers of ivory coloured sycamore and peach velvet curtains and furniture of pale blue leather with white piping produced an atmosphere described at the time as "bright and gay".

The rest of the first class public rooms were situated on the boat and promenade decks, and as the passenger reached the head of the stairs to the main entrance hall on the promenade deck, he would have been met with a statue, by Maurice Lambert A.R.A., depicting two figures in movement, suggesting waves and water. The actual hall itself had two-tone panelling in cream leather and came complete with shops and telephone services to all parts of the world.

Forward of the main hall was a semi-circular observation lounge and cocktail bar which overlooked the bows. The lounge was terraced and the bar itself sunk below the level of the rest of the room. Its walls were of sycamore dyed to a lobster shell colour into which were inlaid scenes depicting circus life. Aft of the hall was another large lounge panelled with Canadian maple-burr of tawny-pink, and having a tall marquetry panel by George Ramon, whose theme was Chaucer's Canterbury Tales. Pilgrims were depicted in a fairy-tale landscape of rocks, caves and trees.

Between the lounge and the next large public room, the salon, was a writing room built around the central staircase, whilst opposite could be found a small area for businessmen who needed to call urgent conferences. The salon itself was a very decorative room with walls of exquisite quilted satin, gilded ceiling mirrors and slender pillars. Facing the orchestra platform was a deep recess in which a wide glass panel showed a detailed jungle scene.

The final first class room on the promenade deck was the large smoking room. A chestnut tree that once grew in the Isle of Wight apparently provided the veneers for this room and from the same tree, Dennis Dunlop carved groups of hunters and fishermen which stood on the after bulkhead. Below the clock there was a large decorative map of

***The observation lounge overlooking the bows (Cobwebs collection) (Above)***

***The main lounge, featuring George Ramon's marquetry panel (Cobwebs collection)(Below)***

*The first class saloon (Cobwebs collection) (Above)*

*The raised terraces of the garden lounge (Cobwebs collection) (Below)*

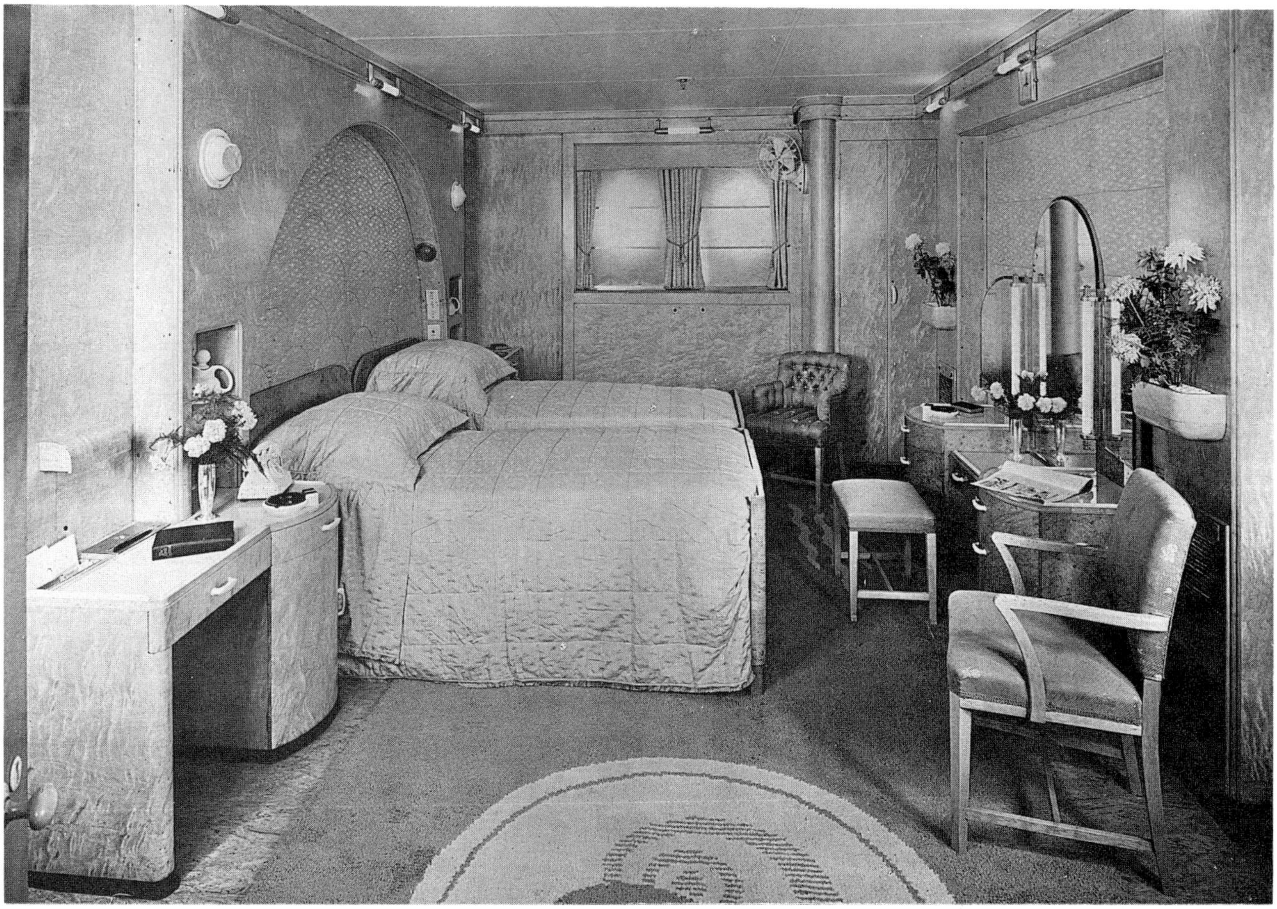

***Bedroom of a private suite – first class (Cobwebs collection)***

***The first class cinema (Cobwebs collection)***

the Atlantic on which passengers could watch the day-to-day movements of models of the Queen Mary and Queen Elizabeth across the ocean. On each side of this room were the raised terraces of the garden lounge, where the passenger swapped the comfortable leather chairs for cane furniture and, surrounded by flower boxes, took tea while gazing out through tall windows at the sea far below.

The first class cabin accommodation was situated amidships on A and B decks, the main deck, and forward of the sun and promenade decks. The Queen Elizabeth carried 850 passengers in first class and excepting the special suites consisting of dining room, bedroom and bathroom, all were staterooms for one or two passengers with telephones, some even had toilets and bathrooms.

Many recreational facilities were provided on board and in addition to numerous deck activities there were three gyms and two swimming pools. The cabin class pool on E deck was lined with golden quartzite and the sloping edges and underwater kerbs were bright blue, with walls featuring a mother-of-pearl-like compound into whch Hector Whistler designs had been placed. The surrounding columns were faced with mosaic-coloured tesserae in cool shades ranging from deep ultramarine blue to emerald green. The first class pool was even better appointed. It was situated on C deck and surrounded by several rooms with exotic names: the frigidarium, tepidarium, calidarium, laconicum, massage room and vapour room. The ship also had two cinemas, one shared by cabin and first class passengers, seating 338, the other for tourist class, with room for 130.

The Queen Elizabeth was to become a beautiful ship, both externally, and eventually internally, but before being given her adornments, she was forced to serve her country in a way that was, when she was first conceived, quite unexpected.

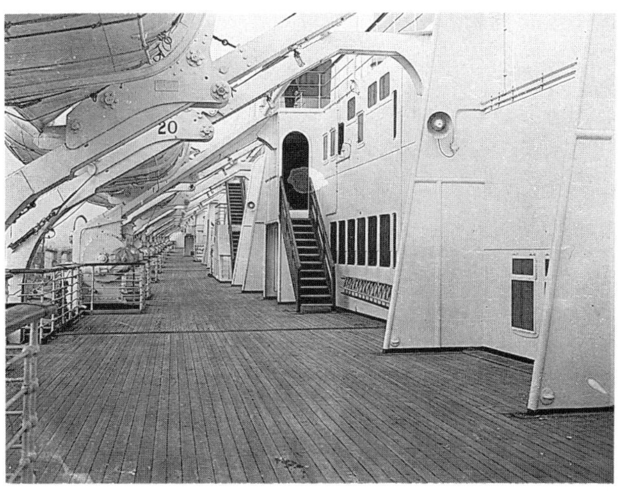

***An idea of the length of the new Cunarder. The view looking along the sun deck (Cobwebs collection)***

***The beautiful liner that she was eventually to become (Cobwebs collection)***

# IV

# All Aboard~ Free of Charge

While the Queen Mary was making a routine Atlantic crossing to Southampton on August 23, 1939, Germany was signing a pact with the USSR. The atmosphere of fun and excitement that usually filtered through the ship was replaced by one of tension, with most of the passengers expecting to hear, at any moment, that war had been declared. The fact that the ship was blacked-out at night, and that it was prohibited to walk on the outer decks after late afternoon didn't help matters, and neither did the suspension of BBC news broadcasts, which were replaced by bulletins relayed over the Queen Mary's own public address system.

Unknown to the passengers, the battlecruiser HMS Hood was shadowing the liner across the Atlantic. During the day, she kept her distance, and then, under cover of darkness, closed in to provide protection in case of possible attack. The liner reached Southampton on Monday, August 28, with Britain still at peace. Consequently, Cunard continued with their schedule and over 2,300 passengers embarked bound for America, on August 30. The news of the outbreak of war came on Sunday September 3, with the ship still at sea. On reaching New York on the 4th, the Queen Mary was immediately laid-up, because it was reasoned that she was too valuable and easy a target for Luftwaffe for her to risk a re-crossing to Southampton. This made her future very uncertain until the small working party that had remained on board were ordered to paint the exterior of the ship grey; it looked as if the Queen Mary was going to war.

Parliament didn't like the idea, still feeling that the ship was too costly to be risked, however, the ministry thought otherwise and at 8 pm on March 1, 1940, they contacted Cunard White Star to advise that the Queen Mary was to be requisitioned. Within a few days another giant grey liner had joined the Queen Mary, and as the newcomer sailed up the Hudson River, New Yorkers got their first look at the Queen Elizabeth.

The Queen Elizabeth had left the Clyde bound, or so everyone thought, for Southampton. As expected, word of this voyage had got back to Germany, and the Luftwaffe bombed Southampton expecting to obliterate the brand new liner and destroy national confidence. But she was nowhere to be found, instead she was heading into mid-Atlantic under the utmost secrecy. Even the crew were apparently unaware of the new destination until the very last moment, with anyone who didn't volunteer for the voyage being kept locked up until the ship was safe in the States.

To further fuel rumours, it was made known on Clydebank that the Queen Elizabeth was bound for Southampton and to authenticate the hoax, the graving-dock at Southampton was made ready for the ship and fittings were sent to the city prior to her supposed arrival. The crew of 500 men were signed on for a short coastal voyage only, and most

***The Queen Elizabeth's life began with a secret dash across the Atlantic (Cobwebs collection)***

convincing of all, the Southampton pilot went on board on the Clyde to take her the last stretch of her so-called coastal journey.

On the new ship's arrival, a telegram was received from Her Majesty Queen Elizabeth, it read: "I send you my heartfelt congratulations on the safe arrival of the Queen Elizabeth in New York. Even since I launched her in those fateful days of 1938, I have watched her progress with interest and admiration. Please convey to Captain Townley my compliments on the safe conclusion of her hazardous maiden voyage."

After a couple of weeks, the Mary sailed south to Cape Town and then on to Sydney in Australia. Her arrival there was a surprise, as were all her subsequent movements in the war – apart from a select few in the high command. The ship remained in Australia for two weeks and underwent the conversion from super liner to super troopship. She had an extra kitchen fitted, stores and more sanitary arrangements whilst some of her exquisite furniture was taken ashore for storage.

Her first wartime task was to take 5,000 Anzac troops to Gourock, and to achieve this, the Queen Mary had been fitted-out to carry up to 5,500 passengers, an increase of over 3,330 on her transatlantic capacity a few months earlier. But there were serious problems. The Queen Mary was never built to operate in hot temperatures and consequently there was no suitable air conditioning. This led to extreme discomfort which apparently caused riots on board, and even resulted in some unfortunate deaths from heat exhaustion as the ship travelled through the Indian Ocean.

In Singapore, the Queen Mary was dry docked after delivering troops to help the garrison's defences, and whilst docked, the opportunity was taken to fit some basic armament and overhaul her major machinery. This proved to be the first of two dry-dockings in Singapore whilst she was running a shuttle between Sydney to Bombay or Trincomalee from where her troops headed for the Egyptian deserts.

In the spring of 1941 there was only one front on which the British troops were fully at grips with Axis forces, in the Western Desert. Small and comparatively ill-equipped Empire forces faced the larger armies of the Italian Dictator and re-inforcements were urgently needed. To fulfil this requirement 11,600 Australian soldiers were taken on board the two Queens in Sydney harbour. The sister ships were joined by Cunard's new Mauretania carrying 4,400 New Zealand troops and they sailed in convoy for the Middle East. At the time the ships were reasonably safe from attack, as Japan was yet to enter the war. Minefields did not exist in deep waters, and for the greater part of journeys, the vessels were out of range of land-based bombers. In addition, their speed made them reasonably safe from submarines; however, when the Japanese

***The Queen Mary rams her escort vessel, HMS Curacao (Author photo of a painting by Harley Crossley)***

attacked Pearl Harbour in December 1941, that danger was magnified many times.

Around this period, it was felt that Australia was in danger of invasion because most of her troops were fighting elsewhere, and so it was decided that American soldiers should be landed there. The Queen Mary was detailed for the task and sailing out of the Indian Ocean, arriving in New York on January 12, 1942. Over three weeks were spent there upgrading the carrying capacity of the ship yet again to 8,500. Standee bunks, often up to five deep, were fitted wherever there was any available space. The Queen Mary was back at sea on February 18 bound for Sydney via Trinidad where stores and Bill Bisset, her new captain, were waiting. At the last moment however, Trinidad was considered too dangerous as an intermediate destination because German U-boats were known to have infiltrated the area. Consequently, the ship was diverted to Key West in Florida and anchored off for Bisset to join her.

Bisset's first voyage was full of drama which began when a ship just ten miles astern of the Queen Mary was torpedoed; the German naval command had offered a financial reward and the Iron Cross to the person who could sink either of the Queens. To further fray nerves, the Queen Mary experienced a serious fire on board that took two hours to successfully extinguish. Luckily the nearby U-boats were unable to keep pace with the ship and the grey, heavily laden liner eventually arrived safely in Sydney on March 28.

When she made it back to New York, her Captain received new orders that were to take her back into more familiar waters. Reinforcements were needed in Europe, and the Mary sailed for the first time ever with a total of over 10,000 troops on board. However, just as the crew got back into the

North Atlantic routine, the ship was ordered away once more. This time she was headed for the Suez via the Cape in a bid to reinforce the Allies against Rommel's Egyptian attack. This trip was made by 9,357 troops and the run was the longest to date – 6,200 miles. This resulted in more deaths from heat exhaustion, especially on entering the Red Sea.

When the Queen Mary returned to New York once again in late June, she had a brief respite before sailing again on the 2nd of August with her largest contingent ever, 15,125 troops which, with the crew, totalled over 16,000 passengers in all. This forced "hot bunking," where sleeping arrangements were shared; when one man left his bunk, another took his place. During the trip to Gourock in Britain, the ship narrowly missed an acoustic mine which exploded close by as the Mary zig-zagged past.

These trips across the Atlantic were carried out at the fastest possible speeds, usually with a cruiser meeting the ship off of Ireland and escorting her into the dangerous home waters. This afforded aircraft cover, whilst up to six destroyers would handle the submarines. Normally things went very smoothly, but on one occasion, this wasn't to be: HMS Curacao was a 4,200 ton cruiser, detailed to act as escort vessel. When the smoke from Mary's funnels appeared over the horizon, the cruiser's Captain had to make haste – even at full speed, the liner would soon overtake the small ship. That day, both ships met off the Northern Irish coast at a spot known as Bloody Foreland. The Queen Mary was executing her zig-zag path which meant steaming straight for four minutes, then making a 25 degree turn to starboard for eight minutes, then fifty degrees to port for eight, then finally a 25 degree turn to bring her back on course. A complex manoeuvre that, from an onlooking ship, could appear extremely confusing and unpredictable.

The Curacao, perhaps not quite reading the zig-zag carefully enough, steamed too close to the Queen Mary's starboard side. Sources suggested that the natural interaction between the two vessels pulled the cruiser directly in front of the Mary's rushing bows. On board the troopship nothing was felt except for a slight jolt as the liner smashed through the cruiser as 28½ knots. Tragically, something much more severe than a jolt was felt by the Curacao, which was instantly sliced in two. The stern section sunk almost immediately closely followed by the bow, claiming the lives of 331 men with the ship's commanding officer, Captain John Boutwood among them: there were only 101 survivors. Troops on the Queen Mary threw lifejackets into the water in an attempt at rescue as the liner steamed on. She was under orders not to stop for anything that could put the lives of the 15,000 troops on board at risk. The collision had cut the Mary's speed by half and her bows had been split and forced back to one side. Fortunately this had the effect of sealing the worst of the damage from the incoming seas, and she made Gourock safely at 14 knots, leaving her escort destroyers to rescue the survivors of Curacao. The bow was temporarily repaired with cement for her return to the States, where after being dry-docked in Boston, a new stem section was fitted.

Following this tragedy, the Queen Mary was used mainly for ferrying American soldiers across the Atlantic. However, in between these voyages, she was called upon to make a passage which subsequently became known simply as the "long

***A troopship deck scene aboard Queen Mary during the war (Russ Finley photo courtesy of Wrather Port Properties)***

voyage". She departed from New York on December 8, 1942 and didn't return until June 16, 1943. In that time she travelled to Gourock, Freetown, Cape Town, Aden, Suez, Australia, back to Gourock, then finally to New York once more. The round-trip measured 46,865 miles, and led to the ship carrying 45,614 passengers.

Up until August 1944, apart from one trip to Halifax in Nova Scotia, the Queen Mary was mainly employed in carrying many thousands of troops, and on several occasions, Sir Winston Churchill too. He travelled under the name of Colonel Warden and after the war, when the Mary alone had carried 810,730 passengers and covered 661,771 miles, he issued the following tribute: "Built for the arts of peace and to link the Old World with the New, the Queens have challenged the fury of Hitlerism in the Battle of the Atlantic. At a speed never before realised in war, they carried over a million men to defend the liberties of civilisation. Often, whole divisions at a time were moved by each ship. To the men who contributed to the success of our operations in the years of peril, the world owes a debt that it will not be easy to measure."

The Queen Elizabeth had played her part too, and once more speed and secrecy were to be the main forms of her defence, with only simple armaments of a couple of pill boxes and some sandbags on the bridge. With a possible speed of over thirty knots, the new Queen Elizabeth could outrun anything that the Germans had on the surface, and the slow U-boats could only mount effective attacks in calm conditions. News of German surface and submarine vessels were broadcast by the Royal Navy, but the main hope for safety, in addition to the liner's speed, was the radio silence that the ship kept. On the first furtive voyage there were only 398 men on board instead of the full crew's compliment of 1,296. During the trip, a menu was printed daily and the crew each enjoyed the luxuries of a brand new stateroom each – this was far from the maiden voyage that Cunard had planned their new liner.

On reaching New York, journalists recognized her, and she was given a tumultuous welcome as she came up the river. Thousands of spectators crammed at the windows and roof tops in every available West Side building, and more than a dozen planes circled overhead, dipping continually in salute. In addition, tugboats churned up the waters on both sides of the great new Queen, filling the New York air with the sounds of whistles and sirens.

The Queen Elizabeth followed the Queen Mary to Sydney after a couple of months, arriving in February 1941 for her refit. On April 9, 1941, the two ships headed for the open sea together for the first time. The stifling conditions that had dogged the Queen Mary were affecting the new liner too, so much so that tempers became frayed and the story goes that many of the crew were on the verge of mutiny at one point. They were fed up with the endless stream of unknown harbours and routes that had turned their ship into a boiling caldron where people were dying from heat exhaustion around them. At one point, the Queen Elizabeth's crew revolted againts the menus and apparently bundled the cook into his own heated oven. He survived, just, but his attackers weren't so lucky. They were rounded up in the lounge, which served as a prison, and a squad of marines came aboard from the escort ship and took the culprits back to Cape Town. From there they were transferred to their English homeland, but only to face strict disciplinary action.

After the boiling temperatures and tempers, the Queen Elizabeth returned to familiar waters with the Queen Mary to begin her job as a GI ferry. Both ships had been handed over to America without payment of any kind and it was left to Washington to decide how to best use the liners. Cunard simply provided the crews and paid them their usual salaries. The British government subsequently re-imbursed this along with fuel, pilotage and any docking expenses. By temporarily giving the Queens away, Britain had lost valuable troop carrying capacity, but this was balanced by the fact that the four American divisions that the ships transported to Northern Ireland in summer 1942, had made a considerable contribution to the successes in the Middle East and El Alamein.

Churchill sailed with the Queen Elizabeth on January 9, 1946, when peace reigned once more, and as the troops headed homeward to New York, 12,314 soldiers cheered the following speech: "My friends and shipmates in the Queen Elizabeth. For most of you it is homeward bound. The seas are

***Queen Elizabeth often carried a whole division of troops at a time (Cobwebs collection)***

clear, the old flag flies and those who have done the work turn home again, their task accomplished, their duty done. What a strange, fearful, yet glittering chapter this war has been. What changes it has wrought throughout the world, and in the fortunes of so many families. What an interruption in all the plans each of us has made. What a surrender of the liberties we prized. What a casting away of comfort and safety. What a pride in peril. What glory shines on the brave and the true. The good cause has not been overthrown. Tyrants have been hurled from their place of power and those who sought to enslave the future of mankind have paid, or will pay, the final penalty.

"Yesterday I was on the bridge watching the mountainous waves and this ship, which is no pup, cutting through them and mocking their anger. I asked myself why is it that the ship beats the waves when they are so many and the ship is one? The reason is that the ship has a purpose and the waves have none. They just flop around, innumerable, tireless, but ineffective. The ship with the purpose takes us where we want to go. Let us therefore have purpose, both in our national and imperial policy, and in our own private lives. Thus the future will be fruitful for each and for all, and the reward of the warriors will not be unworthy of the deeds they have done."

And so war was over, but the Queens still weren't handed back to their rightful owners; they had one more very important job to do. The GI's hadn't only been fighting, they'd been fraternizing as well and there were thousands of British girls who had become romantically attached to the cargo that the Queens had carried across the oceans during the dark days of the war. Attlee wanted to get the British troops home fast and cabled Truman in America, asking for the return of the Queens. After negotiations, the Queen Elizabeth was handed back along with the Aquitania (which had also been requisitioned), while it was agreed that the Queen Mary would carry out the bridal voyages. Between February and May 1946, she carried 12,886 new Americans across the Atlantic, together with 3,678 children. The standee bunks were replaced with cots, nappy rooms and nurseries.

The welcome the ship got with this cargo in New York was spectacular. All the fire tenders were out in the harbour spouting great plumes of frothing water along with tugs and aeroplanes. The authorities had worked out a way to sort everyone out at the other end and herded the brides into wired enclosures according to the State for which they were bound. Following this, husbands were summoned for reunions in alphabetical order, but some just couldn't wait and doors were broken down and the amorous Americans slid down pillars, jumped ropes and became involved in wild scrimages to reach the deafening cacophony of women screaming and children crying. It was the same in Canada until eventually, on September 29, 1946, everyone was in their rightful place, including the Queen Mary, who was now as keen to be "demobbed" as anyone else.

# V
# Getting there is Half the Fun

When the Second World War was over, the Queens between them had carried over one million servicemen. Evidence of this could still be found in the deck rails which had been carved with many of their names. For a while in the mid-forties, these reminders remained, but Cunard was never a sentimental company, and soon they were removed as part of the major refurbishing of the two ships. Cunard had to look to the future, as the sister ships would be spearheading the company's survival plans.

A rumoured thirty tons of paint were required to return the Queen Elizabeth to her rightful Cunard colours, replacing the coat of grey that she had worn, following her completion before the war. Whilst this was going on, over one hundred French polishers began working on the interior of the ship and her interior fittings came out of storage including 4,500 settees, chairs and tables, plus 4,000 mattresses, 6,000 curtains and bedspreads, 2,000 carpets, and 1,500 wardrobes. The standee bunks had gone forever.

There were complaints from some quarters at the money being spent on the Queen Elizabeth while rationing was still in force, and luxury goods were still only a distant memory for most of the British population. The arguments apparently got so severe that, at one point, an official report had to be issued regarding the sumptuous feast laid on for the ship's first REAL maiden voyage. It was hastily explained that all of the delicacies had been supplied by America and Canada, and had been carried back across the Atlantic on the Aquitania; it was stressed that Britain had only provided the potatoes and the boiled fish!

The story goes that the ship's doctor was kept extremely busy throughout this voyage curing many digestive problems caused by people not used to all the rich food after the lean war years. The maiden voyage was unfortunately marred by one tragic event, the death of Sir Percy Bates of Cunard, just before the liner was due to sail. He was the man who had made it all possible and he was committed to the ocean in mid-Atlantic, as was his wish.

Whilst the Queen Elizabeth was getting used to her proper role, the Queen Mary was completing her GI Bride trips. Her first post-war "shakedown cruise" didn't take place until July 25, 1947, with her first civilian voyage commencing on July 31, 1947. This heralded the beginning of Cunard's two-ship, weekly shuttle across the Atlantic. It also heralded in the most successful years of the company's history. The passengers loved the ships, and the top-class crews maintained an air of social snobbery almost to the point of being compared with the aristocracy, so much so that it was said that rich lady passengers would sometimes curtsy to them. A place at the Captain's table was the ultimate goal for social-climbing passengers and also for businessmen who could afford to buy the

***The Cunard publicity slogan launched in the fifties (Cobwebs collection)***

liner out of their own funds! There was evidence of favouritism too, and it was possible for certain influential passengers to phone Cunard the day before the Queen Mary sailed and obtain a reservation in the Verandah Grill for the whole voyage, sidestepping others who had been waiting patiently for several months or more.

Everyone who did manage to secure a ticket for whatever class was entitled to the famous Cunard cuisine. There were often strawberries flown from California, watermelons from Florida, lobsters, snails, caviar, grouse, salmon and more. It was this plus a painstaking attention to detail that made the ships so famous: everything was taken care of. There was even a ship's gardener on hand to water the plants, a feat that meant he had to get out of bed at dawn each morning and embark upon a long trek around 12,000 flowerpots.

Throughout voyages there was plenty to do and for most passengers each day began with a discrete knock on the cabin door by the steward or stewardess carrying a tea tray. After rising, breakfast was served in the dining room, often with a choice of up to eighty different dishes including eleven types of cereal, plus more tea, this time from either Ceylon, India or China, together with five different sorts of toast. This was all served up with a copy of the ship's own newspaper which had been printed on board during the night.

Following the first meal of the day there were opportunities to play shuffleboard, or perhaps use the swimming pool. For the less energetic, a stroll

***After the war, things soon got back to normal on the Queens. (Cobwebs collection)***

around the decks culminating in a visit to the purser's office to buy a sweepstake ticket, could total the morning's activities to make stomach-room for the five course lunch. The afternoon could be passed either working-out in the fully-equipped gymnasiums, wallowing in the turkish bath, sitting in the cinema, shopping in the arcades, listening to the symphony orchestra on board or simply praying for good weather in the chapel or synagogue.

Dinner was a lavish affair on both of the Queens, and the ritual for many affluent ladies commenced with queueing outside the purser's office, waiting for their turn to claim the jewellery that they had left in the safe. Meanwhile, the men often engaged themselves in pre-dinner drinks which were very much a part of the Cunard service, with both ships being equipped with over a dozen bars. The crew weren't left out either – they had a couple of their own too.

Passengers were really pampered, and if there was nothing that they liked on the extensive menus, then they were invited to detail their own requirements. Some tried to make this task impossible for the Cunard chefs, and there is a story of one American oil magnate asking for rattlesnake steaks for four. His order was taken and soon afterwards his party were apparently served eels in silver salvers by two stewards shaking rattles. He saw the joke and the kitchens, as usual, had tried their very best to please.

Extravagance was the name of the game, but perhaps not on such an altogether grand scale as the pre-war years had seen. In the forties and fifties it became apparent that even the richest people no longer required such large suites. Before the war, it was reported that Count Rossi of Martini Rossi booked a suite of twenty cabins. After the war, the largest request was said to have been for twelve rooms, by Sir William Rootes, the car manufacturer. Even Kings made do with smaller accommodation: King Peter of Yugoslavia had a simple Royal Suite which apparently consisted of just three rooms, plus a bathroom and pantry.

For all this, some things continued unchanged, and Cunard were happy to provide little luxuries. There are several stories to support this, for instance, the Marquis and Marquise de la Falaise being given exactly the same suite with identical furnishings every time they crossed: a bedroom steward is rumoured to have taken great pride in remembering each detail. Furthermore, Mrs Fern Bedaux, at whose chateau the Windsors had been married was said to have insisted that lilac scent be sprayed around her suite before she arrived, and the Duchess of Windsor herself always sent advance details of the colour schemes that she wanted throughout her suites.

For such attentions, the stewards of the era could expect tips exceeding £50 per trip, and often used some of this ready cash to tip pantrymen to ensure that their particular passengers got the quickest service. It was a complete circle, with the pantrymen consequently tipping the chefs so that they could supply their tipping stewards.

The premier social excitement of the era was the Duke of Windsor's abdication, and on his first return to England after the war on the Queen Mary, the Captain apparently noticed that the hymn for the Sunday service was "Crown Him With Many Crowns". This was tactfully changed at the last moment. When the Duke travelled he always watched the bellboys attending roll call at seven-thirty in the morning, and finished his day by visiting the bridge for a few minutes before retiring.

The twelve years following 1946 were excellent for Cunard, as a great share of the prosperity was theirs because they had the finest and most famous ships afloat. Both the Queens were always fully booked and that was something that the Queen Mary had never been before the war. In fact, in 1949, the Queen Elizabeth's tourist berths were sold out for a year ahead, her cabin class for six months, and the first class for two months. Because of this, if any passenger wanted a particular first class cabin,

***Menu cover from the verandah grill (Author photo of Cobwebs collection)***

***Embarkation brochure from Cunard's golden era (Author photo of Cobwebs collection)***

then a deposit was required six months in advance of the sailing date. All this meant that the ships were each making profits of around £100,000 per voyage, and, in 1949, Cunard realised a gross profit before tax of £7 million. For three years running, the Queens between them brought in an annual profit of $50 million.

On November 17, 1954, Her Majesty Queen Elizabeth, the Queen Mother, joined the Queen Mary in New York to journey home. She had made a similar crossing in the opposite direction three weeks before on the Queen Elizabeth. She visited the Verandah Grill which had been turned into a

***The premier social excitement of the era centred around the Windsors (Cobwebs collection)***

***The Queen Mother often visited the Queens. This particular photo dates from June 1948, where she is accompanied by H.M. King George VI for a luncheon appointment. She is being greeted by Captain Ford. Mr Bates, the Cunard Chairman is on His Majesty's right (Cobwebs collection)***

temporary TV studio, where she made a speech to the American public. Everyone who met the Queen Mother seems to remember her ability to make everyone around her feel completely at ease. The officers were expecting her to want to take things quietly after her hectic visit to the States, but they were wrong. Instead, she saw as much of the ship as possible and watched the crew carrying out their

***Queen Elizabeth entering New York harbour (Author photo of Cobwebs collection)***

***Throughout the fifties, both ships were well patronised by the rich and famous: (Photos from the Maurice Barnes collection except where credited otherwise)***

***The Kennedy's (Cobwebs collection)***

***Elizabeth Taylor announcing the sweepstake on Queen Elizabeth***

various duties, even meeting many of the passengers at a special children's party. On her second evening at sea she dined at the Captain's table in the centre of the main restaurant, amidst a bevy of ladies all trying to out-glitter each other. The Queen Mother apparently liked the cinema and Geoffrey Marr, who was then the Staff Captain, was detailed to tap on the door of the Royal suite and tell Her Majesty that they were "ready for her now". In this way, she could miss the trailers that preceded the film.

By 1958 the first jets were flying across the Atlantic, but Cunard weren't concerned because 1958 was also the year in which more passengers had crossed the Atlantic on the sea than any year before, and, as it turned out, any year after, either. Cunard reasoned that the ship was still THE way to travel, the company chairman delighted in recount-

***Anita Ekberg***

Diana Dors

Eddie Fisher with Debbie Reynolds

Robert Taylor with Ursula Thiess

Victor Mature

ing a conversation that an American travel agent had when he tried to sell an elderly couple an air ticket to London. The couple simply said: "We've waited twenty-five years to make this trip, and we're certainly not interested in getting there in any six and a half hours!" Stories like these simply strengthened Cunard's resistance to any major changes in the face of the new competition. Every possible reason that the Cunard board could think of was used as excuse for the inevitable gradual decline in the Company's fortunes. They just didn't seem to realise that the only way to make money was to ensure that their ships took on a dual purpose role – cruising in the winter months, and crossing the Atlantic in the summer. No one seemed to take any notice of the fact that stevedoring charges were

***Jayne Mansfield***

***All the time the ships were in port loading or discharging freight, wages were paid out to a catering department for doing nothing. However, the ships were always a fabulous sight at Southampton's busy Ocean Terminal (Cobwebs collection)***

continuing to rise, and it was becoming uneconomical to carry passengers and freight in the same ship, something that had been bringing in much needed extra revenue. Money was being wasted wholesale: all the time the ships were in port loading or discharging freight, wages were being paid out to a catering department for doing nothing.

Suddenly, the ships found themselves trying to cash in on a rapidly vanishing life-style of grandeur and opulence that throughout the fifties and sixties was becoming more and more scarce. The battle against the airliner was one which Cunard never had any hope of winning, and gradually their customers began to drift away from the sea for the speed of the air. Twenty eight knots didn't seem very fast compared with the several hundred miles per hour!

The mid-sixties saw the Queens in serious financial trouble. They really needed to be full of passengers to generate the atmosphere for which they had become renowned, but now many cabins were empty and at times staff outnumbered passengers. Often it was possible to take tea in the grand salons of either ship and be completely alone, except for a dozen white jacketed stewards. As John Malcolm Brinnin wrote, "Not even the dining room in 'Citizen Kane' was emptier."

One problem that Cunard did solve was the rolling of their ships. The Queen Mary had always been notorious for this and one traveller, Paul

***Deserted decks on the Queen Mary during an Atlantic Crossing (George and Joan Caws collection)***

***It wasn't always rough on the Atlantic, as this photo of the Queen Mary approaching New York shows (George and Joan Caws collection)***

***Baggage label (Author photo of Cobwebs collection)***

Gallico, used this design error as the basis for his novel which was later turned into the successful feature film called "The Poseidon Adventure". It revolved around a badly rolling superliner that capsized after being hit by a tidal wave. It wasn't so much this that prompted Cunard to fit stabilisers to the Queens, but the fact that paying female passengers were terrified of the ships in bad weather. With the stabilizers, invented by Sir William Denny, a roll of ten degrees could be dampened within seconds. Special brochures were printed to reassure the worried ladies, and the slogan "To Smooth Your Way Across the Atlantic" was used for the first time.

Cunard's principal motto for the jet age stated simply – "Getting there is half the fun". Unfortunately, there was a double meaning attached to the statement. Getting there could indeed be rather less than half the fun of flying across the Atlantic in a few short hours. With the choice of a trip across the often very rough Atlantic Ocean lasting for four queasy days, or a flight of less than half a day across the same stretch of water, most people were choosing the latter. To make matters worse for Cunard, the competition wasn't only considerably faster, but was cheaper.

1964-5 were dismal years for Cunard, and Geoffrey Marr relates in his fine book, *The Queens*

***Souvenirs remained popular throughout the ship's careers, and many items were produced, including these attractive sweet tins (Author photo of Cobwebs collection)***

*and I*, a conversation with a shipping correspondent in 1961 who was about to interview Sir John Brocklebank, after he took over as Cunard chairman: "The correspondent knew a great deal about most of the large shipping companies, so I asked him how he saw Cunard's future. He said: 'I think Cunard still has a future, but things are in a hell of a mess and it could take at least five years to get rid of the dead hand of Colonel Bates (the ex-chairman). He boasted that he had never set foot in America, but he hoped to get 60 per cent of his business from there, and he had only twice been on board the Queen Elizabeth, the largest unit in the fleet. His idea was that he and a couple of cronies could run a worldwide shipping company from his fifth-floor office in Liverpool'".

The new chairman tried to find solutions to the problems, but each balance sheet showed worse results than the one before it. Cunard were fast finding themselves with a fleet of ageing ships, most of which were totally unsuitable for the money-making cruise business. Added to this, there were constant demands for wage increases, but the line knew that if they put the fares up to cover these escalating costs, then the few passengers that had remained loyal would desert them forever.

To pile on the problems there was a wide gulf between shore based and the sea staff. There were more than 600 people employed in the Liverpool office alone. In 1965 the company's recently retired chief accountant broke down the figures for a balance sheet, and out of the revenue earned by the fleet, a considerable percentage totally some £6 million went in maintaining the company's shore-based establishments. Furthermore, reductions in the size of the fleet didn't seem to be resulting in similar reduction in the size of the shore staff. Commodore Geoffrey Marr, when asked to attend a meeting on time and motion in early 1965, said: "In my opinion, there is only one way in which the efficiency of the Cunard Line can be improved; that is by finding some way of breaking down the barriers that have built up over the years between the sea staff and the shore staff; between those of us who go to sea and do the job, and those people who sit in office chairs and try to tell us how it should be done, often without having any clear knowledge of the problems invoved."

The Cunard management decided that perhaps the answer to their problems was to transform the ships into cruise liners. This kept Cunard solvent

***A more recent addition to the growing collection of memorabilia is this Coalport plate (Author photo of Cobwebs collection)***

***Strolling minstrels, fancy dress and cheap cabaret, as grandeur takes a back seat on the Queens (Ron Macey collection)***

for another few years, and throughout the sixties, the Queens were filled with holidaymakers. The grandeur gradually began to take a back seat, to be replaced with strolling minstrels, fancy dress, and cheap cabaret. It all had an air of a British holiday camp, like Butlins.

At one point Cunard even allowed the Queen Mary to be chartered by a newspaper, *The News of the World*, as a prize for winners in a competition in which entrants were required to place in correct order of merit the eight things that they would most enjoy on a cruise. It was to be a Merry Christmas trip, but it turned out to be a nightmare, with winds gusting well into hurricane force. At one point, the sea lifted the top off of one of the big ventilator cowls on the forward end of the promenade deck and sent it smashing through the promenade deck windows, injuring a passenger and his three-year-old son. Perhaps this was a way that the powers-that-be had of signalling their disgust at such a cheap use for such a grand old lady!

In the 1960s the press which had so often praised Cunard for the engineering and opulence of the Queens, suddenly turned against them. Unkind, but nevertheless true stories began to appear. Magazines ran headlines such as "Cunard-on-Sea" which compared the deserted massive ships to the similarly deserted holiday resorts in rainy English summers. The story goes that one journalist who travelled one way on the Mary and the other on the Elizabeth, criticized the ships by saying that the tourist class decorations reminded him of the

"Winter Gardens near Blackpool", and the crew seemed helpful "in an Ealing Film sort of way". He said that they were "courteous at all times, but always their best in an emergency". He maintained that the best way to obtain service was to be seasick from the moment that you boarded. He also commented that he wanted to bath his children, but the bathroom doors were locked. When he called for the stewardess, she in turn called for the lady bath attendant, who in turn, finding out that the child was male, insisted that she must fetch the male bath attendant. After a further wait, they all had to go down to the deck below where the male bath attendant's bathroom was situated.

The same jaded journalist grumbled that the wine waiter had never heard of a carafe even though it was mentioned on the menu and the bottle that he ordered instead didn't arrive until after the meal. In addition, there were apparently complaints reported from some First Class passengers about the decline in the famous Cunard service. It was said that some stewards didn't even speak English and sounded "more like a foreign football team" – comments like "do you want something to get you drunk?" didn't go down at all well with the handful of First Class faithfuls that had remained true to the oceans.

The Queen Elizabeth was overhauled with an outlay of £1¼ million in 1966 which included the fitting of air conditioning. When the ships were built in the late thirties, air conditioning was almost unheard of and when this was installed to their public rooms it really was an innovation. Everything was fine as long as the ships remained in cool waters. The system was never designed for blue water cruising and during the refit, Cunard had decided to leave the original system in the public rooms and just add the new air conditioning to the rest of the ship to save money. The old system worked on the cooling power of the sea water but when, in the Equatorial currents this rose to over 87 degrees, it just didn't work, and the temperature in the restaurants and public rooms soon became unbearable. It was made to feel even worse because the rest of the ship, which had the new system installed, was deliciously cool.

During the Queen Elizabeth's major refit private showers and lavatories were added to every cabin, together with a new lido deck and swimming pool. But the work didn't go as smoothly as was originally planned: Whilst the ship lay on the Clyde she was subjected to the dubious tradition of pilfering by the workers. Whatever had happened to the pride-in-the-job craftsmen who had built her? Pieces of copper piping were ripped out and sawed into lengths that would fit up trouser legs, then panelling replaced on top of the gaps that were left. This resulted in widespread flooding as soon as the water was turned back on, and as the leaks were hidden behind panels, problems were time consuming and difficult to trace.

What's more, after four months at the yard, not one single cabin was finished. When the chairman was lunching with officials at Clyde it turned out that he wasn't going to be shown the unfinished sections. Geoffrey Marr, who knew that he was going to have to cancel the first planned cruise plus about three voyages, insisted. As it turned out the work still wasn't finished on time and when the ship sailed from Southampton for an Atlantic crossing followed by an Easter cruise to Bermuda, a large section of the ship was still completely empty. There wasn't even a framework of cabins in place. Because of this, thirty workmen were on the ship when it sailed, but progress was still slow – perhaps they were enjoying the cruise. As the ship headed for New York, twenty cabins became flooded and with more than 1,200 passengers booked for the cruise, coupled with the lack of completed cabins, there was no alternative accommodation to offer. Luckily the crew managed to dry everything up and provide new carpets and curtains. Amazingly nobody complained; it's not surprising that the latest refit on the QE2 was carried out abroad when stories like this came to light!

It was only the useful intervention of a seaman's strike at Southampton that provided time for the work to be completed. But if the strike had been good for the shipfitters, it certainly wasn't good for Cunard because in less than two weeks the whole of its fleet was tied up. There were some estimates that it cost the company $4 million when they could ill afford to lose anything. Another unfortunate consequence was that rival foreign competitors had stepped in and taken much of Cunard's forthcoming passenger traffic.

The Queen Mary didn't enjoy a refit like her sister as she was now being considered too old to undertake as vigorous a cruising service (although she did operate for a time between Southampton

***The Queen Elizabeth in the sixties – maritime nostaglia and nothing more? (Cobwebs collection)***

and Las Palmas). Cunard had lost over fourteen million pounds in the preceding five years and North Atlantic sea travel was very much on the wane. It had peaked in 1957/8 at just under one million passengers but had been dropping steadily ever since. To add insult to injury, all the major air companies were ordering the much heralded new "Jumbo Jets". There was still a big demand for winter cruises but Cunard still insisted on "showing the flag", and dragged the Queen Elizabeth away from potential lucrative cruise markets into expensive North Atlantic crossings, where she often ferried no more than a handful of passengers.

It was expensive to fuel the big Queens and Cunard was becoming desperate to gain help wherever they could. The Midships Lobby on the Queen Elizabeth featured gaudy commercial displays and the ratio of staff to passengers dropped dramatically. But it wasn't only the staff that were trimmed; the menus suffered as well. To be brutal, in the sixties, all the Queens could offer was maritime nostalgia. The awesome size of their interiors was still breathtaking for first time travellers, but there had been a lot of cosmetic changes made. The main deck square, Rialto and Plaza was plastered with advertising hoardings. The twin-level observation lounge which had for many years afforded a sophisticated view of the great bow plunging into the waters of the Atlantic had been converted into a simple pub. The old ballroom had gone altogether, replaced by the Midships Bar. There were ugly brown stains from the main deck to the waterline, and flaking paint was very much in evidence. The brasswork was not what it used to be either and instead of the sparkling golden colour that it had been decades before, it was now green and oxidized.

Even so, there remained, for a time, a few traditional delights to cosset the intrepid traveller. These "things" were the handful of "old school" stewards who, in the original Cunard tradition, took great care over their passengers. Paradoxically, it was the passengers themselves that forced these excellent staff members to eventually head for the shore forever. Passengers that were used to motels and self-service became annoyed at being forever fussed around, consequently the last bastions of the age old service soon began to drift into oblivion.

These employees were replaced by new staff who worked for the money alone. To them, working on the Queens was "just a job" and most didn't care much for their passengers and weren't impressed by the flash of banknotes and potential tips. Meanwhile besides, high society was laying low. The grand old Queens had become little more than unique venues for holiday weekends and booze cruises. It was all very sad.

In the end business efficiency experts were called in, but it was all too little too late. They stampeded through all departments and made sweeping but largely ineffectual changes. The Cunard reins were handed to Sir Basil Smallpiece who made further alterations and introduced younger people into the higher echelons of the company to see if Cunard could be steered away from bankruptcy. In a bid to improve matters, the head office was moved down from Liverpool to Southampton which allowed easier contact with the passenger ships themselves, and the staff were trimmed by fifty per cent. But it was obvious to those remaining that nothing could save the Queens now.

# VI Working Passages

The recollections of those fortunate to have lived and worked on the Cunard Queens provides us with a unique perspective unavailable elsewhere. I was lucky enough to be given the opportunity to speak to a broad cross section of crew members in the course of my researches. A considerable amount of the tales that they related provides a valuable insight into the ships from the inside. Here are their stories.

Tom Grant worked as a seaman on the Queen Mary, rising to the rank of Quartermaster. He recalled that it was always difficult to get a job on board: "There was very rarely any change of crew," he said. "If you saw one new face per trip it would be an event; Donald Sorrell, the skipper during my time on board created that. He had a lot of respect for seamen in particular and if he found the stewards' accommodation dirty when he inspected it, he'd say, 'if you don't clear it up, then I'll send the seamen down to do it, and you'll pay out of your own wages.' It always worked!"

Tom was on the Queen Mary in 1955 and then again ten years later. He noticed considerable changes after a decade:

"In '55 my duties would include painting and washing down the ship, working amongst the passengers and ensuring that everything was done with regard for their comfort. You had to be careful where you trod, as the decks were littered with passengers keen to soak up any sun that was available. In 1965, when I returned and was carrying out the same activities it was a very different story – you often had to look twice to find any passengers at all – it was like a ghost ship."

"Furthermore, Cunard had introduced a new rank called UDH; uncertificated deck hand, which allowed unskilled people to work on board. In the mid-sixties, there was quite a large number of these people on board, and that, together with the lack of passengers, was the beginning of the end. I remember having to splice some ropes down in the first class swimming pool, looking forward to it and thinking that I would get a swim. However, when I arrived there the pool was empty. I asked the attendant why this should be and he told me sadly that there were no passengers left to use it any more, it said it all."

It was apparently a joke among crew on the Queen Mary who maintained that when the ship was built, they forgot to put in any crew accommodation. The quarters were considered to be poor by many who worked on board: The Able Seamen used to sleep up in the bowels of the ship and when she pitched and the bows crashed down into the waters, the sound was deafening. In heavy seas, the Mary would rise from her bows and as she reached the top, she'd quiver and shake, which in turn caused the anchor chains used to rattle. The noise produced was eerie, just like the bell on a church ringing alongside the bunks.

*"In 1965, you had to often look twice to find any passengers – it was like a ghost ship" (George and Joan Caws collection)*

On the crossing from Southampton to New York, the ship usually pitched, which meant that seamen slid up and down their fore and aft bunks. One minute their heads were crushed against the head of the bed, the next, their feet were taking their complete body weight at the bottom – however, at least there were rails on the side to stop them falling out when the inevitable rolling started. All the seaman's cabins had a porthole, often having up to eight berths to a cabin. There wasn't enough room for tables and chairs, but there were showers and washrooms.

The stern on the Queen Mary carried the crew's bar, the Pig and Whistle. Here vibrations were so severe that the beer, which in 1955 cost a shilling a pint, was said to dance across the table uncontrollably. The stewards' accommodation was deep in the stern nearby – apparently they always got the worst accommodation but the best tips! They also enjoyed the best food and could often be found amongst piles of plates, tucking into "surplus meals" that had mysteriously arrived direct from the galley that served the passengers.

The longest corridor on board the ship was one which the passengers never saw. It was called the working alleyway and stretched almost the full length of the vessel. "Every thirty feet, you'd have to pass through a watertight door. Off the working alleyway there was the crew's galley. That was the first galley you came to, then, if you went on down, you'd find stewards' accommodation that carried twenty-four bunks. The deck was normally battened down at sea because it was not sufficiently above the waterline for safety. The portholes and deadlights (steel covers fitted on the inside of the portholes) were closed and when the weather got really bad, an order from the bridge was given and a bridge boy was sent around the ship with a piece of paper which had to be signed to say that he'd ensured that the deadlights were secured. If it was getting rough during the night, then the watch were often taken off of what they were doing, and had to go around shutting all the deadlights with a special key. You could often wake up in the middle of the night by a loud clunking as someone shut your windows up."

There used to be a film show run on the Queen Mary especially for the crew. This was projected onto a makeshift screen onto one of the large shell doors in the side of the ship. The screen was fixed up against the inside of the door itself and some chairs set out in front of it, with a shilling being charged for admission. Forthcoming movies were advertised on little notices stuck to the wall of the working alleyway.

The daily sweepstake was always popular with the passengers, but it now comes to light that the outcome wasn't always fair, as one crew member recounted: "The passengers were invited to guess how far the ship had travelled the previous day and figures were always worked out at about five to twelve. I can remember a certain person leaving the bridge with the correct figure, running down to the purser's office and placing a 5/- bet which resulted in him receiving a considerable sum. Cheating wasn't allowed of course – but nevertheless, it did go on."

Bad weather was always a real possibility on the Atlantic crossings, and there was important work to be carried out when adverse conditions were imminent: "The radar would provide you with advance warning of bad weather and as soon as it had been detected, the order to rig the rolling lines (ropes for passengers to hang onto in heavy seas) was called. All heads of department such as the chief steward, chief engineer, etc., had to sign a document to say that they'd heard the directive, then the bosun or bosun's mate would give an instruction direct. That order was considered to be as important as a submarine commander calling dive–dive–dive! You had to work fast because by the time you had got all the ropes out, put the stanchions up and shackled them all along the decks, you'd often already be hitting the approaching bad weather. And when she rolled – she ROLLED! I can remember being at the wheel of the Queen Mary when she rolled well past 22 degrees. The worst trips for rolling were those returning from New York, this was because you had a following sea. In fact, a lot of the movement depended on how skilled the Quartermaster was. It was his job to look out of the wheelhouse, observe the approaching waves and be ready with the wheel to take whatever action was necessary to maintain course. This was all very fine on a head sea, but with a following sea you couldn't tell what was coming from behind, so it was necessary to feel the pattern that the sea produced and work from that, which was considerably more difficult."

Tom Grant recalls that the vast majority of passengers never gained their sea legs on rough voyages: "Just behind our crew accommodation, when I worked on the bridge, was the tourist class. There was a staircase that ran from our deck right up to the funnel deck which the Quartermasters and seamen used to gain access to the area in rough weather. If the ship had been rolling heavily then you could bet that it would be littered with passengers sitting on the steps with very green faces. It smelt dreadful and it was one of the steward's most feared clearing-up jobs. You could always tell that there were suffering passengers in the staircase as you walked towards it because the wind came down from the deck above carrying a terribly unpleasant odour on it."

The Queens were always kept spotlessly clean with deck maintenance carried out whilst at sea during the hours of darkness. The eight to twelve watch in the evening had the job of washing the working alleyway with wooden poles fitted with rubber squeegees. Once that job was satisfactorily completed the men were finished for the day and placed on stand-by. At midnight the watches swapped and the twelve until four gang came on duty. Their principal job, often in freezing conditions, was to clean the outside decks with lime using electric scrubbing machines. On completion of this task it was time for "black pan" – a favourite term for breakfast which, for them, took place at around two in the morning. Sometimes the night watch were over-eager for their food: "I remember doing the deck one night when the ship was pitching slightly. I was running towards the bow with the big electric scrubber, looking foward to my black pan, when the ship suddenly pitched downwards. The heavy scrubbing machine took control and I whizzed off down the deck, smashed into the bulwarks and badly injured my arm. It's when things like that happen that that you're reminded of the power of the sea."

The North Atlantic could be a very forbidding place even when you were on a thousand foot liner, as the following first hand accounts can testify: "There was a terrific height from the bridge to the waterline on the Lizzie, but I can remember the seas coming right over the bridge when she pitched down; all of a sudden there would be nothing around you but frothing white foam that broke over the deck above the wheelhouse that carried the direction finding gear. However she would often plough on through that angry sea at twenty knots or so until things got so bad that the Captain had to reassess the situation with regard to the comfort of his passengers."

"I was on board when the Queen Mary blew all the portholes on one side of the main saloon which was eighty feet above the waterline – and that was with the deadlights up, too! The stewards had thousands of gallons of water to clear up and the ship was turned as much as possible to bring the weather away from her damaged side whilst emergency repairs were carried out. However, the main saloon was completely saturated and I remember looking through the door while the ship was still rolling and watching a huge wave sloshing from one side of the room to the other. There was a row of about fifty stewards along each side of the saloon with dustpans, buckets, and anything else that they's been able to find, scooping up."

I've heard stories that stewards and seamen didn't always get on particularly well with each other. Apparently this was due to the fact that the catering staff would often be given substantial gratuities – often up to £300 on a one-way Atlantic crossing. This consequently created considerable jealousy at times. However, the stewards did have to work very hard almost round the clock looking after the aggravating whims of passengers.

One of the Queen Mary's most interesting escapades occurred when she became involved in an Atlantic rescue on January 29, 1955. Tom Grant, a bridge boy at the time, was handed this message:

TWO SEAMEN FALLEN FROM TWIN DECK TO HOLD NUMBER TWO STOP THEY MORTALLY WOUNDED STOP PLEASE ANY SHIP WITH DOCTOR. This is his first hand account of the drama that followed.

Three hundred and twenty miles from the Queen Mary aboard a 7,100 ton Panamanian freighter called Liberator, two injured men were suffering from a lack of proper medical assistance. Captain Sorrell considered the situation – apparently there were other ships closer to the Liberator but none had the extensive hospital facilities plus two surgeons that we possessed, so he made a decision to change course and go to the ship's aid. The Queen Mary reached the Liberator at 1.30 am on the following morning in a moderate wind. Captain Sorrell ordered the searchlights to be switched on and manoeuvred the Mary into position between the smaller vessel and the wind. Senior First Officer Leslie Goodier mustered a crew of volunteers including the ship's junior surgeon Dr Timothy Yates. Everyone was thanked personally by Captain Sorrell on the bridge before boarding one of the smaller seaboats that were on davits immediately aft of the bridge. They were lowered the eighty-five feet to the sea below whilst some oil was pumped out in a bid to calm the swell. The Quartermaster got the ship's head to wind and a sheltered lee was temporarily created, although the ship continued to roll rather heavily. In the rough seas the little boat took over eleven minutes to bob across to the freighter, and apparently, although I couldn't see, Dr Yates leaped from the boat and scrambled up a rope boarding ladder before being hauled aboard by the freighter's crewmen. The lifeboat was forced to return to the Queen Mary because there was a danger of it capsizing and the crew were suffering from bad seasickness by this time. On reaching us they gained access up a rope ladder that was hung from an open shell door on C deck.

When he got back to us on the bridge, Goodier reported that it would be impossible to get the men off in the conditions that were prevailing at the time. Captain Sorrell acted on his Senior First Officer's report and radioed the Liberator, asking Doctor Yates if he was prepared to stay aboard – he wasn't and said so, adding that the Liberator's crew were ready to lower the injured seamen whenever necessary. The Captain called us together and we decided that it was unsafe to send a boat across again. He was about to radio to the ship once more telling the doctor that he would have to stay aboard when our Chief Officer, Lt. Commander Phillip Read, offered to attempt the second crossing if Captain Sorrell would agree to a new volunteer crew.

After further consultation this was agreed, even though we all knew that the operation would be both difficult and dangerous, and that it relied on split second timing for it's successful outcome. The plan was for the Queen Mary to be brought as close as possible to the Liberator, with the liner broadside to provide the boat crew with a brief lull in which to lower the wounded men into the lifeboat. It was risky, as a large ship stopped in the ocean is difficult to manoeuvre and can easily drift sideways out of control. Anyway, I watched as Read and his new crew were lowered and bobbed like a cork through twenty-five foot waves to reach the Liberator. With the boat in position, Read used a signal lamp to alert us and as quickly as possible, the Queen Mary was eased alongside the freighter to act as a shield. It was successful and for a few moments the Liberator lay in relatively calm sea. Doctor Yates and the two injured seamen were lowered into the lifeboat and as soon as this was achieved we manoeuvred away with only about fifty feet to spare.

First of all they tried to get the injured seamen back in through our shell doors but it was impossible so they brought the lifeboat up to the falls (the two wires that the boat lowers on). Lifeboats on the Queen Mary were never designed to return to the ship, and with the liner rolling about it was a very difficult task trying to get the falls hooks back on. However this was eventually achieved after about five minutes. The lifeboat had an iron bar skate down its side to protect it as it slid down the side of the ship on launching, and this started to take a beating when the lifeboat was hauled up the side of the Queen Mary – seventy feet or so below the bridge, it was getting a very wide swing before it crashed into the ship's side. Read, unprepared for the first impact, was thrown overboard into the sea and it was only the quick reactions of an able seaman yanking him back, that saved him from the waves as the lifeboat continued up the side of the ship.

I could see the boat shuddering and the seamen

were having trouble holding the two injured men steady. To make matters worse, as the boat was hauled higher up, the fall wires started getting hot and began splitting across the pulleys. I was standing next to the winch, certain they weren't going to make it. There were calls of, "stop lifting", "lift away", "stop again" and so on as Captain Sorrell tried to arrange for the boat to be hauled-in between the worst of the swings. When everything seemed to be going reasonably well, the skate dropped off leaving the side of the lifeboat unprotected. This resulted in it collapsing as it battered the Mary's hull. When it eventually reached the level of the promenade deck, Captain Sorrell ordered the winch secured and arranged to have everyone pulled in through a window on the deck. The lifeboat remained shackled there until it was lowered down with a crane in Southampton. The unconscious injured seamen were taken to the ship's hospital and then on arrival in port, transferred to Southampton General Hospital where they made a full recovery.

The passengers, many of whom had stayed up to watch the rescue, organised a collection for the lifeboat crew, which resulted in each man receiving twenty five pounds – equivalent in those days to about a month's pay. In addition, each of the volunteers were given a testimonial on parchment for their efforts. On a lighthearted note, one of the rescuers couldn't find his teeth and assumed that they'd been lost over the side of the lifeboat. Co-incidentally, Captain Sorrell's son was a dentist and a new set was provided free of charge directly the ship got back to Southampton – but it turned

***The Queens had two captains – the staff captain was responsible for the social side of things, especially useful in bad weather, when the captain was occupied for long unsociable periods on the bridge. This particular photo Shows Commodore Maclean on the Queen Elizabeth's navigating bridge approaching New York harbour in July 1961 (Cobwebs collection)***

out that the seamen had left them in his cabin after all!

The youngest members of staff on board the Queens were the bell boys, recruited as fifteen year olds. Often their "cuteness" meant that they were given the most substantial tips. Peter Indge was one of these youngsters who were crammed in with eleven other bell boys in a cabin down in the stern of the Queen Elizabeth right next to the propeller shafts. He explains how he came to be there: "My father went to Cunard House with me and after being vetted I was sent to sea school for six weeks where I learnt how to serve people, lay tables, make beds and respond to discipline. After this I returned to Southampton and signed-on, ready for Cunard to send me on the ship of their choice. I was lucky in that my first ship was the Queen Elizabeth. However I was reprimanded almost the instant we left the quay – I should have been on station but I couldn't resist seeing the ship leave. My first job was in the radio room; there were two of us and when a telephone call came in we had to page the relevant person and take them to a telephone booth. It was simple enough – I just went round the whole ship hollering at the top of my voice. There was a tannoy but Cunard preferred the personal touch of the bellowing bell boys at the time."

Bell boys were often given important duties to perform as in their uniforms they exuded the most appeal. Peter Indge recalls meeting an important member of the Royal Family on the Queen Elizabeth: "Being the smallest of all the bell boys at the time, I was detailed to collect the donations in the ship's church on Sundays. On this particular day, Her Majesty the Queen Mother was present – she used to travel on the ship quite often in a main deck suite of six cabins. The stewards had shown me how to approach her and I bowed whilst she placed a five pound note in the silver plate that I was carrying."

Although bell boys didn't have to do any heavy work, they weren't always happy with their lot and there were some jobs that were hated more than others: "The most boring job was being on the doors outside the restaurant three times a day, opening them every single time someone went in or out, hundreds of times in total. However, this was balanced by the tips that you were given – the Americans were particularly generous and in fact I had a lot of offers of adoption; I've still got the address of one family who were serious about it and tried very hard to persuade me to come home with them to Chicago. They promised that I would have no school or work to contend with, they just wanted me to live with them as their son because I was 'so cute' – I had to put up with that all the time and used to just grin and bear it – it was often well worth it!"

Bell boys' gratuities often exceeded the tips given to much more senior members of the catering staff and sometimes waiters twice the age of bell boys would approach them for loans. It was very rare if gratuities didn't exceed the pay packet on a trip: "On one particular trip in 1955 I was on the cabin class restaurant doors, and made $140 and about £20 – and that was just one way to New York! I remember being the Chief Steward's bell boy and being asked to deliver a pile of invitation cards to an on-board cocktail party. I was supposed to hand them over to the bedroom steward, but instead I knocked on the passenger's doors and delivered them personally. I'd simply say 'You're invited to a cocktail party,' and they'd reply 'Lovely,' and dig in their pockets."

The class divisions were very much in evidence when Peter Indge was working on board, however, along with the other eleven bell boys, he was given the run of the ship: "We had special keys that enabled us to get through gates that separated the different classes, although we had been known to let people through for a gratuity."

Because of their age, bell boys finished work at four o'clock. The day was usually rounded off by a swim in the first class pool, a privilege not afforded to any other member of staff on board. After helping the pool attendant clean up, the bell boys visited the pantry to claim an urn of cocoa and a plate of sandwiches. This was free but apparently the pantrymen was never very keen to hand these items over, as the rest of the crew were required to pay for this service. However Peter explained that most of the crew paid the cooks at the end of each trip to ensure that they got the same meals as the first class passengers.

Next door to the bell boys cabin on the Queen Elizabeth was the Commis waiters' accommodation. These were trainee catering staff who helped the experienced waiters in the first class restaurant and delighted in bullying the bell boys. Peter takes up the story: "They would come into our cabin and issue orders like, 'You – two cokes and fifty Woodbines, Now!" and you had to go. If you didn't you were in their cabin for what they called a Kangeroo Court Case, and you were always found guilty and punished. But I wasn't only the waiters that you had to contend with. I remember being initiated by the other bell boys; they shoved me into a locker which had a few tiny holes in and then lit cigarettes and blew the smoke through. I was trapped in there for what seemed like a lifetime and by the time they opened the door I could hardly breathe. I thought that was it but then they stripped me off and boot polished me all over and forced me to run a gauntlet of pillows – but if I was fifteen once more, I'd like nothing better than being a Cunard bell boy all over again, it was great fun!"

Ron Macey had the unique opportunity of sailing on the maiden voyages of all three of Cunard's Queens. He was originally on Cunard's Cape boats, but that meant voyages of six weeks. Tiring of this, he put in for a transfer to the Atlantic runs which was successful and led to a job on the new Queen Mary. "On the Mary's maiden voyage I was working in the pantries, and that was go, go, go," he explained. "The pantries were in a 'U' shape and we handled toast and teas and coffees. The waiters rushed in constantly expecting an immediate service – their tips depended on it. It was worth it because at the end of the voyage they tipped us for our efforts. For most of the catering department it was always the same – you'd get substantial gratuities at the end of the voyage but half of it was used up paying off everyone who had indirectly helped you to achieve them in the first place."

After working in the main pantries for a time, Ron applied for a job in the smaller deck pantries and was successful. These were spaced out amongst the passenger accommodation and were designed to allow passengers to ring through direct for an even speedier response to their requirements. Apparently this was fine for simple requests, but if one of the passengers required something unusual then the steward would have to rush all the way down to the main galley – which could be almost half a mile away. The story goes that it was virtually impossible to get an elevator, so it was a case of negotiating at least four flights of stairs with a loaded tray. The catering department staff were invariably quite fit!

Eventually Ron worked his way up through third and tourist class until he became a first class waiter. It was hard work: "In first class we would have to look after six passengers between two of us. In cabin class there used to be up to ten and in tourist there was always at least twelve. However it wasn't as bad as it sounds because as you went down in classes the menus reduced accordingly. It was terrible in rough weather – we used to pour a jug of water all over the table before putting the place settings out in an effort to make them stay there a bit better. During the war I was on the Queen Elizabeth and I recall during one storm seeing an enormous pile of nurses, doctors and troops all in one enormous bundle on one corner of the restaurant where they'd slipped and ended up after a sudden roll. Rough weather was the scourge of the catering department as it made their job considerably more difficult. The limited arrangements for storm conditions weren't particularly successful either:

"Restaurant chairs used to have a rope connected to them which could be hooked to special shackles in the floor, but I've seen those snap off completely in bad conditions. As for the tables, they had a little lip that you could flick up; but it was hopeless, everything used to simply tumble over the top of that."

Rough weather could be frightening, not only for the passengers but for the crew as well. Ron recalls one singular event that has remained in his memory: "It was about two o'clock in the morning in mid-Atlantic and I was asleep when suddenly all the lights went out and the ship felt as if it was about to go over. The clothes lockers came crashing off of the walls and my bunk was ripped from its mountings. I really thought that we were going down; no one could see a thing and I was on the floor half asleep and smothered by bedding. The ship seemed to be shuddering and going through the most severe roll that I'd ever experienced. However, after a few moments she came back onto an even keel again. It's hard to explain, but we all had a lot of faith in her."

Cabin portholes would often face the powerful

***Advertisements like this in the mid-thirties ensured that the Queen Mary was packed with passengers – a daunting prospect for Ron Macey (Author photo of Cobwebs collection)***

# "Queen Mary Holiday Tours

**AMERICA & BACK IN A FORTNIGHT**

**FROM £37 5s.**

including ocean fares, hotels, meals, and sightseeing.

Wonderful programme of delightful tours by ocean, river, rail, and lake connecting with all sailings, including those of Britain's Masterpiece, "Queen Mary." The tours vary in length from a few days to several weeks, and cover not only New York, Niagara Falls, Quebec and Montreal, but also Far West points, including San Francisco, Los Angeles, Vancouver and Jasper Park.

**N. AFRICA & MEDITERRANEAN CRUISE**

"Lancastria" (17,000 tons) from Liverpool

**SEPTEMBER 5**

Revised itinerary—additional port of call—increased mileage—no change in rates.

**12 days from £15**

*Write for tours and cruises programmes to Cunard White Star, Ltd., Liverpool, London or local agents.*

# Cunard White Star

D

ocean waves, and even as high up as A deck accidents were known to happen as one steward recalled: "I had a lady in rooms on 'A' deck and was summoned by her bell. When I entered the room I was met with a scene of devastation. The porthole had been smashed clean away by the force of water and there was glass embedded in the blanket that the passenger had luckily covered herself with. Even up at that level, you would often see the water swish by as you were moving through a heavy swell."

It wasn't only the bell boys that were offered the chance of new lives away from the oceans. Ron Macey remembers an incident at the end of a transatlantic voyage where he was approached by a middle-aged couple travelling first class: "One chap travelling with his wife got chatting to me during slack periods and after three days he approached me and said: 'We've weighed you up, and talked to you. We like your personality and we'd like to offer you the chance to work for us in the Mid West. We only use the house for the odd weekend with about half a dozen guests. The rest of the time, the cars, the horses and the house is all yours."

This sort of thing was a regular occurrence for the first class waiters and one pair were offered the chance to go to Los Angeles to work for Dean Martin in his restaurant. They accepted and in subsequent years were often seen travelling on the ship in first class – as passengers. I asked Ron Macey what memories he had retained from when the Queen Mary was a troopship: "I used to take my turn at submarine watch but after two hours staring I often found myself imagining that I'd seen things. With the Atlantic breakers creating never-ending patterns together with the pressure I was under, I was certain on several occasions that I'd spotted a periscope."

"I remember one voyage where we were just off the coast of Arran when suddenly our escort ships started going down like flies. A pair of U boats were under the cliffs simply firing away and putting the ships down."

"All in all, the most exciting time for me came just after peace was declared when the Mary was used to ferry the GI brides. I had to look after twelve cabins full of insatiable women – I didn't get much in the way of conventional tips on those trips, but they more than made up for it in other ways!"

Passengers and crew alike felt that the legendary Cunard service was the best in the world after the war. The menus provided excellent choices and featured considerable out-of-season delicacies that were unavailable in shore based restaurants. For the most part, the catering staff were eager to please and nothing was ever too much trouble. The service was efficient and fast: There was an office in the galley which waiters came to with special orders. The person in charge of this, arranged for a chef to commence work on the requirements directly so that the passenger was kept waiting only the minimum time possible.

Working on the Queens wasn't easy and staff were expected to work extremely hard throughout the time that they were on duty. I spoke to a bedroom steward about his career on the Mary and it only served to reinforce this point: "The main job was to do the rooms, which were thoroughly inspected after you had finished. In addition, in first class, you were expected to arrange and run cocktail parties, too. I remember having fifty people in one big stateroom for cocktails, whilst in another of the rooms that I was looking after, there was a party in full swing for twenty – I was run off my feet – I had to get the booze that was required up from the bars and sort out the glasses and the ice. And throughout all this I had to ensure that other rooms weren't neglected otherwise there would have been complaints leading to a severe reprimand from the chief steward. It didn't end there either as the rooms had to be cleaned twice a day. Often passengers would want you to take their clothes to be valeted, arrange for evening gowns to be pressed and even handle their personal laundry. The main requirement for the job was patience. I remember one chap for whom I could do nothing right – when his laundry was returned, he threw it at me saying that it was washed in vomit water."

When the QE2 was put into commission Ron Macey transferred over to her. He considered it a fresh challenge and found a ship entirely different to the old Queens. His first reaction was surprise over the departure from the usual Cunard interior fittings. Apparently a lot of regular customers that had transferred with Ron were and didn't like the new style, considering it to be rather sparse in comparison to what they had become used to on the sister ships. Ron's opinion was based on a much more down to earth assumption: "The ship was carpeted throughout unlike the older ships and I knew that the stewards were going to have

considerable trouble in rough weather cleaning up spills and seasickness problems – I was soon proved correct. We used to work in threes as bedroom stewards on the QE2 — two bedroom stewards – and a stewardess. That worked out fine if you trusted each other and shared out all the gratuities equally at the end of the voyage, but I found one of the team keeping tips for themselves. We all did the same job of work for the same people, it was very unfair."

The majority of the crew considered their accommodation on QE2 to be far superior to either the Queen Mary or the Queen Elizabeth. Many of the stewards were provided with air-conditioned two berth cabins, as opposed to twelve berth dormitories with straw mattresses. According to

***Galleys were extremely large and well equipped – this is what the passengers don't see on QE2 (Author photo)***

***Whilst passengers leisurely board QE2 in all their finery, there is a hive of activity going on down below (Author photo)***

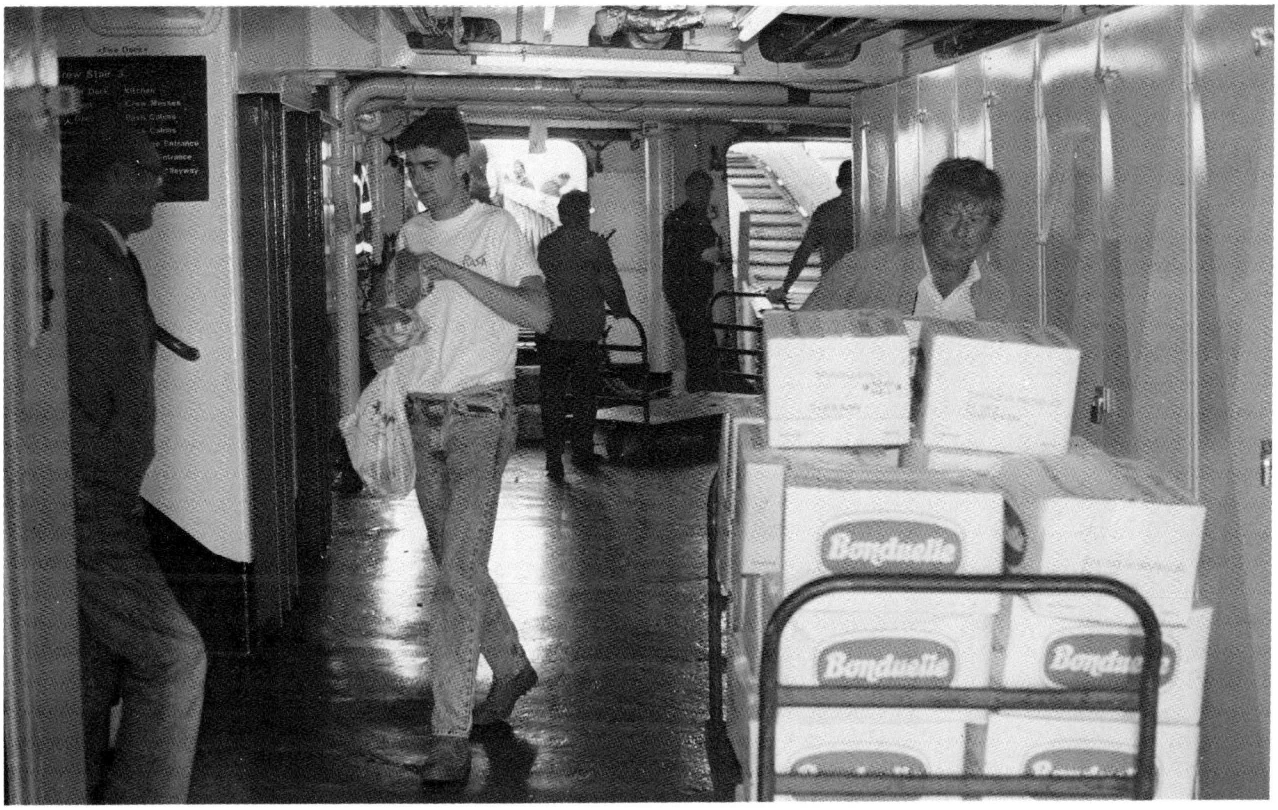

***Captain and officers find time to pose for a photo on QE2 in 1969 (Cobwebs collection)***

Ron, work was generally easier on the new ship: "We had some extra assistance on the QE2 – there were night men that answered passengers' bells and they used to get all of our requirements ready for the following morning during their shift which saved us a hard job. However, there was more time in port when the QE2 began her life. Now it's rush, rush, rush, a turnaround of just a few hours, whereas we used to have two or three days. I don't know how they do it these days!"

Perhaps the staff move even faster in the eighties, or maybe they work out in the QE2's two extensive gyms to keep in shape. Whatever the secret, the QE2 still sails looking immaculate on each voyage.

***This stern area becomes one of the busiest parts of the ship when the QE2 prepares for open sea, and the huge mooring ropes are manhandled by the deck crews (Author photo)***

# VII
# The Sale of the Century

The news that both of the Queens were to be retired before the end of 1968 was hard to believe as they had become such famous British institutions, but with the commencement of the construction of a new cruising Cunarder on the Clyde, it had become increasingly clear that the Queen Mary's days were numbered. She was never treated to the overhauls and reconditioning that the Queen Elizabeth was given and consequently was still unsuitable for the warm water cruising that Cunard was finding necessary to maintain financial security in the sixties.

In contrast however, the Queen Elizabeth, with its new look, air conditioning, lido decks and outdoor swimming pool, fitted in 1965-6, enabled her to operate successfully as a cruise liner when the number of passengers wishing to cross the Atlantic dwindled dangerously low. In addition, when necessary, the Queen Elizabeth could function with the new liner to maintain Cunard's tradition of a two-ship weekly transatlantic service. But the loss of passenger traffic forced a different outcome and Cunard, never being a sentimental company when money was a consideration, made the decision that the Queen Elizabeth must follow her sister into early retirement.

In November 1967, the chairman's message was read out to Cunard crews telling them that, in addition to the two Queens, the Caronia, Sylvania and Carinthia were also going to be withdrawn from service and put up for sale. This meant that, in effect, Cunard itself was up for sale. A decade before, the company had maintained the greatest passenger fleet on the North Atlantic. Now it was reduced to a mere three ships. In terms of employment this meant that 2,700 people would lose their jobs, among them many who had provided a lifetime of service to the company. It was to be a choice of either early retirement or redundancy pay with the official line from Cunard's chairman being: "It is a matter of great regret to the company and to me personally, as it will be to friends throughout the world, that these two fine ships, the Queen Mary and the Queen Elizabeth, must shortly come to an end of their working lives. They hold a unique position in the history of the sea and in the affections of seafaring people everywhere. But we cannot allow our affections or our sense of history to divert us from our aim of making Cunard a thriving company and no other decision will make commercial sense".

It had been a strange move by Cunard to announce the withdrawal of the Queen Elizabeth so soon, especially as she still had a whole season of cruising ahead of her. Some apparently felt that she immediately became "a cheap store that had hung closing down sale notices all over it." However, it did evoke a re-awakening of interest in bookings, with many passengers travelling on the ship for a last time purely for reasons of nostalgia. Conse-

***Queen Elizabeth gets spruced up in King George V graving dock, Southampton in February 1962 (Cobwebs collection)***

quently in her last summer season, the Queen Elizabeth only ever sailed once with less than 1,000 passengers on board and that was a great improvement on the previous year. After this Cunard still maintained scheduled winter voyages across the Atlantic which continued to make huge losses. The ship never travelled with more than 700 passengers on board and the battering that it took from adverse weather conditions made it difficult to maintain the paintwork to the standard required for the money-making cruises.

On the Atlantic run for the summer season passenger numbers were steadily improving and by the time May 1968 arrived, the earnings had overtaken the expenses and the Queen Elizabeth began to actually contribute a profit to the company's balance sheets. When the ship left New York for the last time on Wednesday, October 30, there was a fabulous traditional send off on the clear bright day. The Mayor, John Lindsay, came on board and made a speech which centred around the close connection that both the Elizabeth and the Mary had enjoyed with the city. Following this he presented a plaque from the American government as a citation to the ship's war service, together with a bronze medallion from the City of New York in recognition for the close links between ship and city.

The farewell voyage began as the ship sailed down the Hudson with tugs and fireboats together with all the ships in the harbour, and ended with the entertainments staff and many of the passengers crowding onto the dance floor to sing a rendering of "Auld Lang Syne". Before the final farewell cruise down to Las Palmas, Her Majesty Queen Elizabeth, the Queen Mother, journeyed to the ship for the last time. Prior to her arrival a shore gang hurriedly washed down the exterior on the starboard side and staff made a last effort to polish everything inside the ship. Cunard and British Rail clubbed together and inside the terminal were banks of flowering plants.

All this made the old ship look her glamorous former self when the Queen Mother went on board. After talking for a short while to crew members she was escorted to the promenade deck's Midship's Bar where she was introduced to the ship's senior officers and representatives of the directors and managers of Cunard. Cocktails followed before the delegation moved on to the Verandah Grill for lunch. During this, the Queen Mother expressed concern for the ship's future, hoping that her proud tradition would be maintained. Then after a tour of the public rooms and the bridge, she was gone.

On November 8, 1968, the Queen Elizabeth sailed on her last cruise. It was in fact the first time the ship had begun a cruise from a British port. The destination was to Las Palmas and Gibraltar and there was for once a full passenger list. At Gibraltar the Navy and RAF provided a spectacular send off and the Queen Elizabeth was escorted out to sea by Royal Navy ships. As the Queen built up speed each of these came alongside and saluted before returning to harbour. Whilst all this was going on jet fighters flew overhead.

The Queen Elizabeth returned to Southampton on Friday, November 15, and that night all her crew left for the last time apart from 193, who were going to take her to Florida to meet her new owners. The final farewell in Southampton was very subdued and dawn had only just broken when the skeleton crew took her out into the Solent waters for the last time. The tugs gave the traditional three long blasts on their whistles as they left, but the Queen was unable to answer as an electrical fault had rendered her whistles silent. It was left to the Royal Navy to administer the best farewell using HMS Hampshire, a guided missile destroyer who steamed close to the Queen with her crew manning the rails and cheering the ship. Many people at the time felt that the Queen Elizabeth was being quietly "swept under the carpet".

The welcome in Florida was much more enthusiastic with thousands of people lining the shore and a constant flotilla of yachts, both large and small joining the ship during its final approach. This trip had brought to an end the protracted arrangements that had led to the sale of the Queen Elizabeth and resulted in the decision to bring her to Port Everglades. A strange deal had been signed which meant that the crew were to stand by the ship for nine months after which time she would be moved to a "more permanent berth" and be ready to transfer to shore power. In the meantime, the engine room had to be looked after and the boilers kept in working order. The ship was now owned by a new company that had been registered in Delaware and entitled the Elizabeth Cunard Corporation of which Cunard actually owned 85 per cent of the stock. It was also understood at the time that when the ship was eventually moved then Cunard were hoping to be involved in the proposed development. The most important job for many of the ship's company was therefore public relations, and talks about the ship were given at many club meetings in the Port Everglades vicinity.

During this time no-one seemed to be too sure

***A familiar landmark on the Southampton skyline disappeared forever on Friday, November 15 1968, when the Queen Elizabeth sailed from the Ocean Terminal for the last time (Cobwebs collection)***

what was actually going on and there was concern that things weren't going as planned. Another problem was that the tours of the ship that were being operated weren't even covering the day-to-day expenses that being there incurred. Consequently rumours began to circulate and several affluent businessmen began to express interest in buying the ship. This resulted in a party coming aboard on behalf of a C.Y. Tung, who, as we shall later learn, was to become very much involved in the Queen Elizabeth's final years.

Financial problems were getting so severe that Cunard issued a statement that if the development proposals did not go ahead by the end of July, then she would leave Port Everglades and return to England. This resulted in the crew preparing for the possibility of a long voyage. However the situation suddenly took another turn, a new customer called Utilities Leasing materialized and the bargaining began again.

The Queen Mary's future was much more certain. Cunard had decided that they would rather the ship didn't go for scrap but were nevertheless anxious that the liner shouldn't be placed in competition with their new ship. Therefore it turned out that she was sold to the City of Long Beach, California for $3,450,000. The deal was actually signed on August 18, 1967 and featured a clause which stated that the ship was to be used as a maritime museum, conference centre and unique hotel.

The Queen Mary had earned Cunard £132 million and had cost £5 million to build. All in all she had sailed through 3,790,000 miles of ocean and carried 2,114,000 passengers. She left New York on September 22, 1967, amidst a spectacular farewell and sailed through a two day storm, eventually reaching Southampton on the 27th, her 1001st crossing. During this she passed the Queen Elizabeth and they closed to within one mile of each other for a final brief farewell at a combined speed approaching 60 knots.

Cunard had agreed to deliver the Queen Mary to Long Beach and supply a skeleton crew to do so together with the fuel required to get her there at low speed. The new owners decided that this was simply not good enough and wanted to make the delivery trip into a cruise. This was a questionable idea as the ship was not fitted with air conditioning and there was the danger of having to navigate the potentially hazardous Cape Horn, but still it went ahead and Long Beach made arrangements with agents Furgazy Travel to market the trip as "The Last Great Cruise". This it was hoped would allow the city to recoup some of the $650,000 that the delivery was going to cost. It was, from a booking point of view, a success as 1,093 passengers took advantage of the opportunity and paid up to $9,000 each for their tickets. This gave the organizers an eventual profit on the exercise of $125,000. To look after this unexpected influx of passengers there were eventually 806 crew on board. Right from the start there were problems – everyone was very overworked, and very strong complaints were voiced which eventually led to overtime being paid.

SOUTHAMPTON SOUVENIR EDITION

DAILY EXPRESS

No. 20966 TUESDAY, OCTOBER 31, 1967 NOT TO BE SOLD SEPARATELY PRICE 4d.

**Goodbye to a Queen**



FOR the Queen Mary, majestic old lady, there was this admiring salute from a little girl in red as [illegible] slipped away on her final voyage from Southampton to N[illegible] York. Thousands more will be waving again today as the big ship with its three towering funnels [illegible] England to retirement in the sun.

**It's the last great cruise**

by MONTAGUE LACEY

CALIFORNIA, here she comes! That great ship the Queen Mary sails from a British port for the last time today, on a cruise to the glamour and sunshine of Long Beach, California, 13,260 miles away.

The City of Long Beach has paid Cunard £1,230,000 for her and will convert her into a floating maritime museum and floating hotel.

Last month, as she left New York, there was a tremendous farewell. Now it is Southampton's turn to say goodbye: sadly but affectionately.

at 9.30 a.m. Every ship in port will blow **bon voyage** greetings, and the roar of the Queen Mary's three one-ton steam whistles will be heard above them all as she replies with a three-fold note of thanks, loud enough to be heard 10 miles away.

There will be more than 1,000 dollar-paying Americans on board, making the last great cruise. They will call at Lisbon, Las Palmas, Rio de Janeiro, Valparaiso, Callao (Lima), Balboa (Panama) and Acapulco.

The longest leg of the

***The Queen Mary's delivery to her new owners became a mammoth cruise that she was never designed to undertake – her departure made front page headlines in colour! (Author photo)***

This voyage was to be the Queen Mary's longest since the war, and for it some 4,700 tons of fuel were loaded together with 8,560 tons of fresh water. But even this wouldn't be enough; the Queen Mary had been designed to cross the Atlantic and this was very difficult from the 14,559 mile journey that she was now expected to perform in her old age. Because of this, there were going to be some forced stop-overs for replenishments. The ship sailed on October 31, 1967 to an extensive Southampton send-off. The band of the Royal Marines were playing on the quayside and fourteen Naval helicopters were flying in an anchor formation overhead. As the ship passed Cowes, she received a message from the Royal Yacht Squadron which read "I am sorry to say goodbye, very best wishes."

The first port of call was Lisbon with the first leg of the passage being rough and fairly unpleasant. During this the ship passed the British aircraft carrier HMS Hermes; her company provided a rousing cheer. From Lisbon it was on to Las Palmas where a further 6,000 tons of fuel was loaded on board. As mentioned, the ship was making a slow passage to conserve fuel and some passengers were already getting agitated about this. However Cunard were not going to change their plans as at the reduced speed the ship was only using half the amount of fuel that she normally got through on her Atlantic runs, 550 tons instead of 1,100 a day.

After Las Palmas the next stop was Rio de Janeiro – and the ship's next refuelling stop. Once into the warmer waters the Queen Mary became unbearable and for one very unfortunate crew member, memories of the deaths due to the heat in the war became a nightmare come true; on Monday, November 13, the fish cook, Leonard Horsburgh died of cerebral haemorrhage caused by heat stroke.

The catering staff on board attempted to provide the Cunard service that had always been synonymous with the Queen Mary, but they were

***The beginning of "the last great cruise" (Maurice Barnes collection)***

finding it increasingly difficult as souvenir hunting took hold. It seemed that everybody wanted to take away their own piece of the Queen Mary and by the time the ship arrived at Rio the "Mermaid Bar" had been forced to start using disposable paper cups because so many glasses had mysteriously disappeared.

The voyage was one of the rare occasions when the Queen Mary did not sail as a happy ship. Normally the crew enjoyed their work, but on this voyage they were faced with situations which agitated and aggravated them. One of these took place on Wednesday, November 15, at 11.15 am. Horsburgh, the fish cook who had died so tragically, was given a burial at sea in full view of the passengers. This was arranged by Captain Treasure Jones, who had decided on this particular time of day so that the spectacle could be witnessed by as many of the passengers as possible, giving them an insight into how such arrangements were administered. The crew disagreed strongly with this decision and were very offended when over-eager sightseers began taking photographs of the proceedings.

At such a vast distance from England it became increasingly difficult for Cunard to maintain routine contact with the ship and this meant long delays while the Captain awaited instructions. To avoid these, Cunard decided to hand over full control to Captain Treasure Jones and he was instructed to get the ship there by himself without bothering to attempt to establish further contact. This meant that he was entirely in command and responsible for all his actions. He later said that it was "just like being in charge of a wonderful, beautiful toy that you had to be careful with".

As the ship headed for Cape Horn there was an air of apprehension as no-one was really sure exactly what the weather was going to offer up. In the event it turned out to be cloudy with a moderate north east wind with just a slight swell. However that night the weather began to blow up and by midnight there was a very rough sea and rain squalls – the Queen Mary had been just in time. A stunt was dreamed up by someone on board and passengers queued to board the London buses that had been loaded onto the liner aft of the main deck to say that they'd travelled around the Horn on a bus. The vehicles themselves were provided to transport visitors from the centre of Long Beach to the ship once she was put on display. The proceeds of the "Cape Horn trips" were given to an orphanage in Valparaiso.

The rough seas continued all the way to Valparaiso but the Queen Mary arrived safely to complete the longest leg of her journey – 3,895 miles. Following this she stopped at Callao and then Balbao before continuing on to Acapulco. Champagne cocktail parties began taking place on board which were augmented with caviar and Havana cigars. The reason for these celebrations was mainly due to American import restrictions – no-one wanted to waste good food, drink and tobacco!

Five hundred miles out from Long Beach a DC 9 jet flew low over the ship and repeated the gesture that had been afforded to the ship on her maiden arrival in New York at the start of her career, that of dropping hundreds of flowers – however, on this occasion most of them missed. The Queen Mary's arrival was compared with Beatlemania. The cheers of well wishers drowned all other sounds out as the liner came alongside her berth. There followed a dockside ceremony during which the Cunard house flag was handed over to the Mayor of the city who presented Captain Treasure Jones with a flowered key to the city. On Monday, after clearance of the Long Beach cheque, the American flag was raised to take the place of the British ensign.

# VIII
# 81,000 Tons of Fun

Since her 1967 arrival in the Port of Long Beach, the Queen Mary has stood as one of Southern California's most popular landmarks. She was first opened to the public in 1971, and since that time millions of visitors have taken the opportunity to relive the elegance and luxury of the ship's sailing days. However, the conversion from ship to floating museum wasn't easy.

The first problem was to determine whether the ship was indeed a ship or merely a floating building. This was important because both maritime and land based unions were vying for the conversion work. The Cunard sales contract stated that the ship was never again to be used for trading at sea, but rather would become a maritime museum and hotel, restaurant, shop and tourist complex. In the weeks between purchase and delivery, the City of Long Beach had developed an organization that was composed of ship's experts and city employees, known as the "Queen Mary Project". It was their job to prepare for the ship's arrival and make the conversion plans.

Once the British crew had returned home, the city found itself unable to open the ship to visitors for some time. It did not have the trained personnel that could guarantee the safety and security either of visitors or the ship itself, and the new operators had to become acquainted with the 370 fire stations and hundreds of miles of wiring, together with numerous switch locations and piping controls – all of which had to be replaced.

The original Queen Mary project was made a separate department of the municipal government. Rear Admiral John J Fee (U.S. Navy Retired) was the first director, being formerly assistant and deputy chief of the Navy Bureau of ships and Vice Commander of the Pearl Harbour Naval Shipyard. It was his task to see that his organization co-ordinated all the conversion and operation of the Mary and ensured that the ship fitted the requirements that were laid down in Cunard's sale contract.

The first obstacle to surmount was the removal of 800 tons of residual fuel from the ship together with the cleaning of several dozen fuel oil and other contaminated tanks. It was originally planned to put the Queen Mary in the Naval Dry Dock at Terminal Island on February 22, 1968. Drydocking was necessary for the closing of around 90 underwater hull openings, the removal of three of the four propellers and the construction of an enclosure around the fourth one. From this observation area the propeller would be clearly visible through a large glass floor to visitors within the ship. Other necessary work was the removal of the stabilisers and sandblasting and painting of the underside of the hull, to make it ready for a return to the water. However, because of a jurisdictional dispute between the marine unions and upland unions, the ship was prevented from dry docking for six and a half weeks until finally on April 5, the secretary of the Navy Ignatius issued a directive to the Commander of the Long Beach shipyard to accept the Queen Mary. Work was eventually completed and on Friday, May 17, the ship returned to pier E, the original port of landing, to undergo the rest of her conversion.

Smith-Amelco were the primary contractors and their first job was to gut the machinery areas including five boiler-rooms, two turbo generating rooms, a water softening plant and one of the engine-rooms. One engine-room and the propeller shaft area remained intact as a feature for the proposed visitor tours, the other three were scrapped and removed. One is now in the Museum of Science and Industry in Los Angeles, whilst the other two are adjacent to the ship. The resultant space was originally planned for exhibits and a maritime museum. To make up for the subsequent loss of weight, 8,000 tons of specially treated drilling mud was loaded into remaining fuel and water tanks to bring the ship down to her normal draught.

The plan was to remove the three funnels in sections, lift out the machinery and then replace them. However once the sections hit the pier they fell apart, and on closer inspection were found to be held together by 105 coats of paint. Consequently the installation of the new air conditioning was delayed so long that the new machinery rusted while being stored on the pier.

No maritime conversion work on this scale had ever been attempted before and aside from new air conditioning throughout the ship, all fire, electrical, sewage, telephone and other services also had to be carefully replaced. Nowadays the underwater areas of the ship are protected by a special cathodic system to prevent salt water corrosion.

Originally the estimate for the complete project was $10 million, which included the purchase price, however this was proved to be considerably inaccurate and the finished work ended up costing around $65 million with $20 million of that being used for the ship itself and the remainder going to extend the Long Beach freeway to service the property and to dredge a special berth at pier J directly opposite downtown Long Beach to a depth of forty-five feet.

The original plans for the ship centred around a Museum of the Sea run by the California Museum Foundation. The area was to total over 100,000 square feet of exhibit space and was planned for the six lower decks. There were to be five principal exhibit areas. The first, the "Phenomena of the Sea", would give visitors an introduction to the museum, setting the mood for the rest of the tour. An atmosphere of realism was planned utilising front and rear motion picture projections on the walls and floor together with the unusual lighting effects, wind machines and an 8 channel sound system, which would all combine to give the visitor the illusion of being under the ocean. The second area was to be "Heritage Hall", a room 130 feet long, 85 feet wide and almost 50 feet high. Here would stand a full size 15th century galleon with numerous other exhibits including a carousel of ships and folklore displays. In addition, a variety of deep sea diving gear was on show, and there was to be a special children's museum.

The third area was designated "Highways of the Sea" which would link heritage hall with a further area known as "Horizons Hall". Here a storm deck replica of the bridge was being designed depicting the Mary in the teeth of a hurricane, and also heading into New York in dense fog. The Hall itself was to measure an area half the size of a football field and several stories high. It was to feature ten different exhibit areas which would include an oceanarium. In the centre of this, a large relief map of the world would constantly change through the use of overhead projectors, backlighting and ultra-violet rays. Another planned feature in this section was a simulated trip to the bottom of the sea where 200 people at a time would plunge into the depths.

More interesting for maritime aficionados was to be the Queen Mary exhibition where, after viewing a dramatic biography of the ship, the visitor would descend into the engine room to watch one of the ship's steam turbine engines in operation. One of the housings would be cut away to reveal the inner workings of the last remaining engine, as an electric motor slowly turned the drive. Walking aft along a cat walk, the developers were providing a unique viewing area for the propeller and the plan was to allow visitors into the aft steering station located directly above the ship's huge rudder.

The remaining one-third of the available areas on the Queen Mary were going to constitute the commercial aspects of the ship. After auction this was let under a master lease to Diners Club

Incorporated. Their job was to set up a new division, known as Diners Club/Queen Mary. The upper six of the Queen Mary's decks would comprise the area covered by the master lease, with the Convention Deck, (formerly known as R deck) acting as a focal point. This would feature a magnificent banqueting hall for 1,100 people in the old main dining room. The complete deck was calculated to provide 90,000 square feet of dining, meeting, display, registration and support areas for conventions.

The three decks immediately above the convention deck were to be the hotel area. This was planned to extend to over 400 rooms, with several special suites including entertainment parlours. The entire first class section was being redesigned to make comforts compatible with the best shore-side establishments whilst maintaining the feel of the ship.

The shops aboard the Queen Mary were to remain and were originally planned as two sections, the exclusive high fashion and unique items and the souvenir type goods. The plan for the restaurants was extensive and included turning the sun deck's famous Verandah Grill into a gourmet restaurant. The promenade deck would feature three further choices – the Queen's Dining Room, (ex main lounge) being converted into "an exclusive dinner-dancing attraction designed for evening clientele". On the promenade deck the Long Beach planners has designated an area for their Garden Grill, on the spot where tea was served regularly at 4.00 pm for over 30 years. This facility would serve both day tourists and hotel guests. Finally a King's Tavern was being constructed which would handle "a limited menu in a club atmosphere", with the emphasis being on carved meats served from an exhibition cart. The many bars and cocktail lounges on the old Queen Mary were to be reduced to the Observation Lounge (on the fore part of the promenade deck) and the long gallery bar. These would be supported by self-contained bar areas incorporated in the dining rooms. Diners/Queen Mary planned a full spectrum of entertainment; on the sun deck there were to be strolling bands of

***The Queen Mary in Long Beach, California, next to the dome housing Howard Hughes' all wood 200 ton flying boat, the Spruce Goose (Wrather Port Properties photo)***

musicians such as Highland Pipers and Mariachi groups!

Conversion was well advanced and the opening date just months away when Diners Club pulled out of the project. This meant that Long Beach had to find new operators fast. After frantic negotiations they hired Speciality Restaurants to run the shops and dining facilities, Pacific Southwest Airlines for the hotel and a non-profit group called "Museum of the Sea" to operate the tours on board. Things didn't go well with this split management system which lost around $2 million per year. However, the same arrangement remained in operation for nine years while attendances fell from a first year of 1.5 million to around 700,000 annually. Things took a turn for the better when finally in September 1980, the Wrather Corporation was brought in to take over the management of the entire property. This led to the Queen Mary making a profit in January 1983 for the first time since being brought to the city. To further encourage visitors, Howard Hughes' massive flying boat, the Spruce Goose, was brought to the complex and opened to the public under a purpose built all-weather dome in May 1983. This boosted attendances back to above the million mark where they have remained ever since.

The staff on the entire property numbers around 1,100 which includes Captain John Gregory who, although not an experienced sea captain, still fulfills the traditional role of welcoming important passengers and overseeing the general condition of the ship. He is also an ordained minister and performs around 600 wedding ceremonies each year in the former second class smoking room. Special events now include a nightly fireworks show during the summer, the three day Queen Mary Jazz Festival held each May in the parking lot next to the ship, plus special observances such as the fiftieth anniversary of the ship's maiden voyage and the twentieth anniversary of her arrival in Long Beach, etc. On New Year's Eve 10,000 people visit the ship for a wide variety of live entertainment held in each of the public rooms.

Dining and entertainment these days is well catered for on the ship and there are several outstanding venues. The first is Sir Winston's – a tribute to Churchill. It is the Queen Mary's most elegant restaurant and features California Nouvelle cuisine combined with a view out across Long Beach Harbor. Adjacent to this is Sir Winston's Piano Bar which is open nightly for live music. The Chelsea, another restaurant option also overlooking the harbour, is used mainly for buffet lunches and dinners of the seafood variety. The promenade deck now houses the Promenade Cafe which still has bright art deco furnishings and a casual atmosphere featuring a seafood bar, cocktail lounge, fresh salads, hot seafood entrees and sandwiches. At the stern of the ship can be found The Capstan restaurant. This is exclusively for hotel guests and is nautically themed with a private outdoor deck area for meals or lounging. The Observation Bar is apparently still one of the most popular spots on the Queen Mary and has become an Art Deco cocktail lounge. The table bases, bar area and woods are original and live music can be heard on most evenings. The Grand Salon is still in occasional use too and a Sunday Champagne Brunch is served in its splendour each week. This features a 1,250 square foot buffet with 54 different entrees from around the world. The music here is once again live, this time courtesy of a classical harpist.

***Dining in the ship's "tribute to Churchill" restaurant, Sir Winston's (Wrather Port Properties photo)***

One of the 1988 marketing ideas was the "Queen's Big Bash" where, during the summer months, visitors became "passengers" on a cruise back to the 1930s and 40s. Beginning daily at 4 pm, an upper decks party was highlighted by

***The bright Art Deco styled promenade cafe (Wrather Port Properties photo)***

non-stop entertainment from the era along with shipboard games such as shuffleboard and deck tennis, shopping, food and classic film footage. The ship itself became "the stage for a cast of zany characters that include a torch song singer, spy, villain and man overboard, who involve the passengers in their shipboard antics". The party concluded with a fireworks finale every night at 9 pm along with a re-creation of an old-fashioned live radio show and a musical salute to Irving Berlin and other swing era greats. In addition to this, an eerie flashlight shipwalk known as the Queen Mary Ghost Tour is planned. This takes intrepid visitors on a guided tour into the "spirit filled lower decks" of the ship. On a lighter note, during the day there are barbershop quartets, dixieland bands and the 16 piece Queen Mary brass band providing non-stop music.

Nowadays, the Queen Mary shipwalk tour begins on the lower decks where you pass the first class starboard gallery which has original furnishings placed in a recreation of one of the first class passenger lounges. A few yards from here is the print shop and then it's on to a multi-image show billed as the Queen Mary Story. This depicts the

***The observation bar has remained a popular spot on the ship, and is largely original (Wrather Port Properties photo)***

ship from her launching, through war and peace, ending with her arrival at Long Beach. The historical theme continues with an area called Job 534 that tells the story of the construction of the ship through original photographs and artefacts, with one of the ship's anchors forming the central exhibit. Retracing steps and walking down a flight of stairs brings you to the engine room. Here, the last of the Queen Mary's remaining engine rooms comes to life with a show depicting a fictitious incident involving a near collision at sea. Down another flight of stairs and you find yourself thirty feet below the waterline between two towering propeller shafts. An escalator then takes you up to the emergency steering station. This houses the ship's emergency helms and the machinery which steered the Queen Mary throughout her career. Adjacent to this is the last remaining propeller which is still in position on its shaft. It is viewed from the specially constructed room built onto the ship's hull.

***As dusk falls, the Queen Mary comes to life (Wrather Port Properties photo)***

Continuing is the master model builder's workshop where visitors can watch constructions in progress. One then comes to the Hall of Maritime Heritage which features Cunard's model of the Queen Mary built in 1935. The model is 1/49th actual size and constructed on a scale of ¼ inch to one foot, measuring 21 feet and weighing over a ton. It was constructed from a single log of 200 year old white mahogany from Africa. The log was cut into planks then laminated together for greater strength and to prevent warping or cracking. The model has more than 4,600 individual fittings on it and is on loan from the South Street Seaport Museum in New York. Beside the Queen Mary model is another Cunarder, the Mauretania, together with displays of navigational equipment, knot tying and rigging plus a special exhibit called Ships of Destiny which recounts stories of five famous ships and how their careers at sea abruptly ended. Finally, for visitors who want to take away a permanent reminder of their tour, there is a photo studio that features a Queen Mary backdrop.

After climbing the stairs from the lower decks area you are returned to the main walkway and ride an escalator to the upper decks. From the gangway you pass the Royal Wedding Chapel where over 600 weddings are conducted every year, then it is a short walk across to the aft observation point from where the ship's stern can be viewed with Long Beach harbour and the Californian coastline in the background. Climbing up onto the sun deck there is an anti-aircraft gun similar to one used on the ship during the war. In front of this is an outdoor ice cream and juice bar. The shipwalk continues on the starboard side where a ship's officer recreates a lifeboat drill at sea and also a lifeboat lowering test in port. Access is also available from this part of the ship to Sir Winston's restaurant and the famous Verandah Grill, which has lost much of its exclusiveness now that it has been turned into an area serving hamburgers, sandwiches and family beverages inside or outside on the adjoining sun deck. Also nearby is the "Cool Kiosk" which serves frozen fruit juices and cotton candy.

The tour then meanders along the starboard side of the sun deck which overlooks the 1800 slip downstream marina and village and also central Long Beach itself. The first thing you come to is the Sun Deck Exhibits Entrance which is an area dominated by authentic furnishings from the ship. Inside to the left is a recreation of the ship's gymnasium and next door, the first class children's playroom. You progress down a corridor to the first class drawing room and then come to a section given over to world war two displays. This features sets that show how the Queen Mary was transformed into a troop carrier. After this large section you pass

***The royal wedding chapel, where over 600 ceremonies are conducted every year (Russ Finley photo courtesy of Wrather Port Properties)***

***The captain's quarters (Ellis-Sawyer photo courtesy of Wrather Port Properties)***

the chapel, hospital and barber's shop before proceeding to the bow observation point. From here you can look out over the ship and see a panorama of the Los Angeles river flowing into Long Beach harbour and, on a clear day, the island of Santa Catalina.

From the bow observation point you are led to the port side of the sun deck and climb the stairs to the sports deck. A door near the top of the flight takes you into the officer's quarters just aft of the bridge. This area houses the original Captain's bedroom and dayroom, the Staff Captain's cabin and the Captain's Steward's cabin. Also on display are pictures of many of the Queen Mary's past skippers. Coming back into the daylight through another door you climb a further flight of stairs which takes you into the bridge and wheelhouse. This comes to life with a show depicting activities during a fictitious near collision which takes place in the thirties before the Queen Mary was equipped with radar. Leaving this on the opposite side of the ship you take a flight of stairs down to the sports deck where such activities as tennis, shuffleboard, quoits and golf took place. Walking out across the deck, you approach the Wireless Radio Room. This area contains a variety of original communications equipment and is now an amateur radio station with the call sign of W6RO. Next to this is a section devoted to displays of some more of the ship's original communications equipment including anti-

***A shipwalk tour takes you to the bridge and wheelhouse (Wrather Port Properties photo)***

que radio sets and the old telephone switchboard.

Passing through another door that brings you back out onto the deck, then descending a flight of stairs takes you to the promenade deck to starboard where pictures of many famous people and im-

***Nowadays, the Queen Mary is commanded by "Captain" Gregory (Russ Finley photo courtesy of Wrather Port Properties)***

SLOW
HALF
FULL
STOP
FULL

*The so-called Piccadilly Circus shopping mall was a focal-point on the Queen Mary during her sailing days – a tradition that is still maintained (Wrather Port Properties photos)*

*The luxurious 390 stateroom Hotel Queen Mary is one of the world's most unusual hotels. The ship's uniquely decorated staterooms feature original furnishings and wood-panelled walls (Wrather Port Properties photos)*

portant moments in the Queen's history are displayed, including the story of her final voyage to Long Beach. This area leads to some more stairs towards the ship's bow section. The shipwalk allows you to walk right around the windlasses before passing through a doorway to the Bow Exhibits Room. This houses more authentic furnishings and re-creations of cabins that used to accommodate passengers on transatlantic crossings. Mock-ups of cabin, first and tourist class staterooms can be viewed plus a first class suite and adjoining maid's quarters. There are re-creations, too, of the long gallery and the purser's desk. Before leaving this area there is a candy shop to visit called "Anchors Aweigh", then it's back up two flights of stairs to the promenade deck.

The promenade deck and the so-called Piccadilly Circus shopping mall were focal points of activity on the Queen Mary when she sailed, and this tradition is maintained with the area being used as a centre for eating, shopping, drinking and

***The grand old liner ablaze with colour (Wrather Port Properties photo)***

***With Disney now masterminding the Queen Mary's future, it will be a long time before the ship reaches her sunset years (Wrather Port Properties photo)***

entertainment. The shipwalk around this section commences with a stroll along the promenade deck on the port side where there are pictures of more famous passengers, then it's into the first class main lounge which has been re-named the Queen's Salon. From here you are led to a passenger information terminal where questions about the ship can be answered or you can join a more extensive guided tour. This area opens out on to the shopping mall itself where, together with three nearby restaurant areas – the Promenade Cafe, the Chelsea and the Observation Bar, are a selection of eleven shops stocked mainly with souvenirs to round off your visit.

There's an interesting story of a prediction made by Lady Mabel Fortescue-Harrison, although there's no record that her title was recognised. Lady Mabel, as she liked to be known, was apparently an astrologer in London's 1930's. She prepared a forecast to appear in the leading newspapers on the day of the Queen Mary's maiden voyage. The prediction which seems to have come true began as follows: "Most of this generation will be gone, including myself, when this event occurs. However, the Queen Mary, launched today, will know her greatest fame and popularity when she never sails another mile and never carries another paying passenger."

Jack Wrather had been operating the ship successfully at a profit but was bought-out in January 1988 by the Disney Company. The main reason given for this was that Disney had purchased a nearby hotel and land and were hoping to further expand their operation. The current staff are very positive about the Disney takeover and are currently hosting Disney "Imagineers" who are working to develop long range plans for the ship. Her future now seems assured for many years.

# IX
# The Doomed University

The Mr C.Y. Tung that visited the Queen Elizabeth whilst she was idling in Port Everglades became her eventual owner when he made the best bid in a subsequent bankuptcy sale held by the ship's first owners in mid 1970. From the outset, C.Y. (as he was most often called) realised that he was going to need help getting the ship running, and contacted Cunard's nautical adviser, Captain F. J. Storey, and enquired whether Commodore Marr, her last Captain, would be interested. He was. Consequently he was offered a job for the trip from Port Everglades where the ship lay, to Hong Kong which was to be her new home port. In addition, C.Y. contacted R. E. Philip, who had been the chief engineer on the ship from 1966 to 1968, who also agreed to assist in the project.

C.Y. was a solidly built man of average height, whose features had a habit of relaxing into a warm and friendly smile. He was said to be very enthusiastic, good humoured and had an excellent relationship with all the members of his staff. He was said to be very approachable and even the junior men were able to discuss things with him freely. This was apparently a marked difference from the way things were run at Cunard in that period. The British press carried the following statement about C.Y.'s plans for his new ship: "The world famous passenger liner, Queen Elizabeth, has now been renamed the Seawise University (a play on the initials C.Y.). Lying in Port Everglades, Florida, she is now undergoing a check-up, and the necessary repairs are being done to make her fit for sea again. When she leaves Port Everglades she will follow her old wartime track round the Cape of Good Hope to Singapore and Hong Kong where extensive refitting will be carried out. While preserving her original beauty and elegance, the major work of her conversion will be to make her suitable for the floating campus project now being formulated, and when she sails again it will be with students, faculty members and cruising passengers.

"The ship's new owners recognise the challenge imposed in operating, by today's standards, such an uneconomic ship in an unviable trade. It is to meet this challenge and keep the 'Old Queen' afloat that every possible effort is now being exerted. The Queen Elizabeth is the largest passenger liner ever built and it is extremely unlikely, in this modern jet age, that another ship of her size and capacity will ever be constructed. It is felt that for sentimental and historical reasons that the presence of this magnificent ship in Eastern Waters will arouse much interest and general appreciation. It is also hoped that when she cruises around the world, she will help in promoting mutual understanding and an exchange of culture between East and West. It was for this aim that the Seawise University was named and dedicated, despite the burdens both technical and financial already foreseen. It is recalled that it cost the American government almost 4 million dollars a year to keep the first atomic merchant ship, the Savannah, at sea and she has now had to be laid up.

"To keep a ship of this enormous size ploughing through the oceans is not a simple or light task," said the Duke of Westminster, chairman of the Maritime Trust of London, in a letter to Mr C.Y. Tung praising him for his efforts to save "this fine ship."

The months of shady American sales wangles were at an end and instead of lying in a Florida harbour with an uncertain future, the Queen Elizabeth looked set to continue working at sea. Commodore Marr and Mr Philip signed a contract with C.Y. and then after a couple of weeks they flew to Port Everglades with an ex-repair manager from Thornycrofts who had, for many years, been responsible for the ship's major overhauls.

When they first saw the ship, they were apparently shocked at the state she was in. From a distance the liner still looked her tall imposing self apart from some evidence of extra rust and grime, but once on board, the decay became more obvious. There was dirt and rubble everywhere, most of which had been brought up from the engine rooms and simply dumped in any space that seemed to be available. Efforts were being made to return the engines and hull to a state of seaworthiness but no one had attempted to maintain the rest of the ship. Consequently it looked drab and depressing, a fact which wasn't helped by the almost total lack of electrical power on board.

It was obvious that the sailing date, set for about two months ahead, had no chance of being met. The new Chinese Captain was Commodore William Hsuan, and he was having no end of problems. The crew for the Queen Elizabeth had been drawn from various other vessels in C.Y.'s fleet. Most were experienced to a point but had never even boarded a ship such as the Queen, and consequently had no experience of operating such a complicated and large piece of maritime machinery. It immediately became obvious to Commodore Marr that an extensive training programme would have to be put into operation before the new team could even begin to control the world's largest passenger liner.

The engineering staff on board were despondent and reasoned that the only safe way to get the ship to Hong Kong would be to tow her there. The liner's boilers were in a terrible state after their two years of neglect, but when this fact was reported to the Port Everglades harbour commissioners, they insisted that it was impossible to move such a large ship out into open water without at least two of her main engines providing power. To make matters worse there was 4,000 tons of oily water lying in the engine rooms, and the water separators were in need of repair. There was also a potentially dangerous loss of stability due to the free surface effect of this loose water but no attempt had ever been made to deal with the problem, apart from an abortive try at chartering a little coastal tanker to pump some of it out. This failed, as there were regulations about dumping oil at sea, and so in the end it was finally pumped into an area between the ship and the dockside and then cleaned from the surface of the water using straw.

The language barrier produced considerable difficulties and Mr Philip found it almost impossible to detail engineering problems to the Chinese workers who only trained in shore-based engineering anyway. However, progress was gradually made and at the end of December, two months after Commodore Marr had arrived, the first two repaired boilers were flashed up and worked! Subsequently, two of the main generators were restarted, resulting in electric light being available once. The navigational and radio equipment was ready, too, and this, together with the safety equipment, was carefully checked to Lloyd's standards.

Engine trials were held on February 3 and the ship was deemed ready to sail. But the conditions had to be right and all six tugs from the port had to be available. That meant choosing a day when no other big ships were either entering or leaving the harbour. The day of Wednesday, February 10, 1971 was eventually chosen and dawned cold but clear. Preparations began at 6.00 am when the chief pilot and the six tugs came alongside. The weather was almost identical to conditions experienced when, over two years before, the ship had first docked at the port.

Just as the operation was about to begin, bad news came from the engine room: one of the six working boilers had developed leaky tubes which forced a shut-down. Undeterred, the crew continued with the original plans and the ship began to gradually make its way, assisted by the six tugs and short bursts from the engines. The tugs pulled the ship through the 300 foot wide entrance channel that led to open sea, then full ahead was rung on the telegraph for the first time in over two years. Dense clouds of black smoke billowed from the after funnel as engineers in numbers 3 and 4 boiler rooms did their best and urged the ship up to a dismal five knots before a tube burst in another boiler, releasing water into the furnace and making emergency procedures and a shut-down the only possible course of action.

Seconds before this, Commodore Hsuan had decided to salute the well-wishers that had been lining the shore. The traditional three blasts on the powerful steam whistles were attempted but the pressure was so low that the first blast tailed off to nothing. There was a total lack of power and the liner that had once maintained speeds of almost 30 knots was having difficulty manoeuvring enough to even let the pilot off.

By 10.00 am the ship was on her way once more and achieving 8 knots. Progress was slow but uneventful until it was noticed that the reserve feed water level was dangerously low. As a direct consequence of this, the engineer was left with no choice but to close down number four boiler-room completely. After further complications the remaining ones had to be shut down too. Emergency measures were put into operation and after several hours the ship was underway again at 7 knots. The following morning was ushered in by the jangling of the fire alarms which signalled a blaze in number three boiler-room, the only one still operating. Black smoke billowed through the engine-room skylights and ventilators, and engineers needed breathing apparatus to tackle the fire with foam extinguishers. The outbreak was controlled within an hour but the damage to the boiler was so severe that it had to be completely shut down. Now there was only one actual boiler that could provide any power at all, A3. There was no alternative but to arrange for towing, a decision that caused great disagreement between the British engineers who felt that they could repair and push on, and the Chinese who didn't; As the Queen was now theirs, the embarassing decision stood.

Throughout the ensuing consultations, the ship drifted helplessly for three days. At one point a Norwegian cruise liner passed close by and enquired whether assistance was needed. "No" came the very tight-lipped answer. On February 16 a tug arrived on the horizon and towed the Seawise (as she was luckily now being known) towards Kingston, Jamaica, but the wind changed and the ship began pushing her way towards dangerous waters. For this reason a second ocean tug was requested. This arrived next day and a new course was set, this time for Curacao more than 500 miles away through heavy winds and sea.

The journey took six days at a snail's pace, during which the destination was again changed, this time to the island of Aruba which offered safer and better anchorages. This was reached at a speed of three knots on Wednesday February, 10, 1971, exactly two weeks after leaving Port Everglades on a leg of the voyage which, taking into account the reduced power of the ship, was only calculated to have lasted four days. It was difficult to get the ship into the harbour using nothing more than the power of the tugs and so the anchor was dropped. It turned out that it had lodged on the edge of a steep shelf on the ocean floor but by the time this error had been noticed the tugs were long gone. The ship managed to hold fast for four days waiting for the arrival of salvage officials to assess the damage and decide who was going to carry out repairs.

On the fifth day the wind increased and the ship dragged itself free into deep water, finally re-anchoring four miles away exposed to the strong trade winds. With the ship in this predicament a tug was requested to come to the rescue, but due to a problem with paperwork, the Captain of the tug refused to assist and left. Returning again the next morning, he began towing, but in the wrong direction before radioing to say that he had developed engine trouble. Without another word it uncoupled and steamed inshore. The Seawise was again adrift, this time sixteen miles from land. At this, several of C.Y.'s officials arrived and suddenly the "faulty" engine on the tug was mysteriously repaired. Eventually, another tug joined the first one and the liner was secured at anchorage once more so that repairs could get underway.

The work continued without any real urgency until a senior advisor from C.Y.'s organisation arrived four days later. After technical discussions had taken place it was agreed that a thorough repair job had to be carried out on six of the ship's boilers, whatever the expense. 600 boiler tubes were duly flown in from New York together with other materials air-freighted from England. The planned repairs proved complicated and lengthy and the Seawise University was forced to spend a further eleven weeks at her island anchorage. Towards the end of work C.Y. made a personal visit to the ship which renewed enthusiasm, and more experienced staff were flown in from Hong Kong to replace those that had been frightened off by the boiler room blaze earlier.

Tests were finally completed on Sunday, May 9, but one of the main feed pipes burst and it was another twenty-four hours before a re-start could be made. The next day (exactly three months after she had left Port Everglades) the ship was finally underway once more using her own power. A short trip was made to Curacao where supplies were taken on, then on 13th, the old Cunarder left for Trinidad. The average speed was 8.5 knots.

The Captain and engineers were keen to keep the ship well within her limits to avoid straining the repaired boilers. Because of this, there were only five fires in each instead of the usual seven being very small .28 burner tips, with pressure restricted to 325 lbs per square inch, 100lbs below the normal operating level. Commodore Hsuan was attempting fuel calculations for the trip, but this was proving unreliable, as the ship was in the full force of the equatorial current. Because of this he decided to change course and head out of the Tropics towards Rio. The ship arrived there safely on May 30 to a very warm reception. After a short stopover she was able to leave as planned on a 3,343 mile trip across the South Atlantic, arriving in Capetown on June 13. The ship was afforded excellent news coverage, and the shorelines were filled with well-wishers as she sailed again that afternoon. After rounding the Cape of Good Hope the weather turned cooler, and the ship began rolling in the heavy swell; cupboard doors and lockers banged open and shut in the hundreds of unoccupied cabins. The Seawise University was making slow, steady progress, but the European engineers were depressed — now that the boilers were thoroughly tested they were keen to get the ship running properly. However the Chinese wouldn't agree and the reward for asking was a further speed reduction to just 8 knots.

Arrival in Singapore was on July 7 and during the approach, cargo vessels, which would never have been able to keep up with the Queen Elizabeth a few years earlier, were overtaking every few minutes. The Seawise was escorted by two Shackleton RAF planes, and then, just as the ship weighed anchor, by a formation of six fighter aircraft of the RAF who flew low over the ship, followed by six Royal Navy helicopters. There were no official receptions because the Chinese owners, realizing the ship's shabby appearance, were desperate to keep the vessel out of the public eye until she had at least been repainted.

It was hot and humid when the Seawise sailed once more and made its passage across the South China Sea, with torrential rainstorms only serving to increase the humidity to almost unbearable levels. The plan was to enter Hong Kong harbour on Wednesday, July 14, with a reception arranged for the following day. But surprisingly under the circumstances, the Seawise University arrived too soon and was forced to flounder along at 4 knots; a speed at which it was almost impossible to accurately steer. To waste time the ship spent a day cruising around outside the harbour entrance. Next day, (Thursday, July 15), the ship began threading its way into the harbour through hundreds of tiny fishing junks who were cleared from its path by two army helicopters and a pair of large patrol craft. The fire boat was in attendance and produced the customary water fountain display as the ship docked. News items about the ship made headlines in most of the newspapers and an RAF helicopter touched down for a few moments in between the ship's two huge tunnels. Plans for an extensive refit were already very well advanced, but before cosmetic work could be started, millions had to be spent simply bringing the ship into line with the 1966 IMCO convention on safety of life at sea.

The mood became confident: C.Y. had considerable financial resources and was unlikely to cut corners in returning the ship to first class condition. It was a difficult task but by no means an impossible one. As long as the hull and engines were basically sound then it would be a relatively straightforward matter of tearing out everything that needed replacing. This was much cheaper than building a similar ship of even a quarter the size.

The main problem was of obtaining a suitable loyal crew prepared to stay with the vessel whatever her future held, learning each of her little idiosyncrasies over a period of time until the ship became something that fare paying public would look forward to boarding. This was a complicated problem for C.Y.'s organisation: 1,000 men and

***The maiden voyage of the Seawise University (Ex- Queen Elizabeth) that never was (Author photo of Cobwebs collection)***

women had to be trained to operate the ship and provide a high level of service within a few short months. To make matters worse, even though the name had been changed, the service would inevitably be measured against the enviable reputation of Cunard's Queen Elizabeth. Commodore Marr felt at the time that the standard of discipline on board was not what it should have been, and that, although the Chinese were undisputably hard workers, they were poor at organizational skills.

As it turned out, none of this ever mattered. The Seawise never did become the long white Eastern cruiser; she was engulfed by fire in Hong Kong harbour on January 9, 1972. Prior to this, excellent progress had been made on her refit and all four engines and twelve boilers were already back in full working order. In addition, there were announcements posted in the American press and numerous travel magazines reported a planned inaugural seventy-five-day luxury Pacific cruise. This was due to start from Long Beach, California (eventual home of the Queen Mary), on April 24, 1972.

Sunday, January 9, 1972 was a fine sunny day and so thirty-two shell doors were open on A, B, R and C decks, together with another sixteen on C deck plus numerous portholes. Security guards were in position and although there were sixty welders on board, there was no evidence to suggest that any of them were working anywhere near the areas associated with the subsequent outbreaks of fire. Decks were being swept and scrubbed and in the new Peacock Lounge on the promenade deck, preparations were being made for a large formal lunch party.

Fire was first discovered by three cabin boys at about 11.20 am. They had been sweeping up rubbish on M deck for disposal into a collection barge below, and on their way aft along the alleyway towards the disposal point they saw smoke in the area of a rubbish pile that they had just left. They dropped the load they were carrying and hurried to look, noticing a few small two-inch flames covering a small area of the pile. Instead of trying to extinguish the outbreak, they turned and ran forward shouting "fire". All firemen and fire patrolmen were subsequently ordered to the outbreak and an announcement was made over the tannoy. Shortly afterwards, the public address system went dead and the Chief Officer made arrangements to gather the lifeboatmen and lower the boats, just in case. The shore services were contacted but the caller had some difficulty in making it understood that the Seawise University was a ship and not some institution ashore. Staff Captain Hsu who was in the main restaurant on R deck heard shouts of fire and went up the main stairway where he was met by thick black smoke at A deck in the port alleyway. Reports were coming in of other fires alight in different parts of the ship, one on the sun deck, and another aft on A deck.

From this point onwards the Commodore endeavoured to use A deck office as the fire control centre. By now there was mounting confusion, due in the most part to the mysterious failure of the public address system. Instead of a muster en-masse, individual crew members and patrolmen were given missions to perform as and when they appeared. The Commodore gave Staff Captain Hsu the order to "put steam on the whistles" as he felt that it could

***The crumpled liner rolls over and dies (Cobwebs collection)***

become necessary to sound them to attract nearby craft to assist in taking people off the ship, and also to announce the occurrence of a grave emergency. By 12.10 pm after several pleas for assistance, fireboats were at last on the way. In his evidence at the enquiry, the Commodore said that after he had been informed of the existence of other fires elsewhere in the vessel, he had the "intuition that something quite extraordinary had happened!"

Chief Officer Zee was ordered to begin evacuations and told the security guards to get everyone off the ship other than those engaged in the actual fighting of the fires. After this he went via R deck to the stairway at 70 frame. There he saw a fire burning on the B deck level within the stairway enclosure. The people engaged in the fighting of this fire were being forced back because of dense smoke combined with a lack of breathing apparatus. After retreating down a nearby stairway, yet another fierce fire was spotted further aft in a smaller stairway on the port side. The panelling of the stairway enclosure was alight so a hose was quickly run out of a nearby deck hydrant to begin fighting this new mystery blaze.

Chief Officer Liu Hen, having left the useless public address system, made his way to the bridge in a bid to switch off the ventilation system to reduce draught in vulnerable areas, but when he got to the boat deck he found thick black smoke in the wheelhouse. He opened the door and rushed in. Finding the ventilation system off, he clambered down some workmen's ladders to P deck, spotting a lot of smoke in the port alleyway as he hurried to join the Commodore at the makeshift fire control centre. On arriving he was ordered to return to the bridge to sound the general alarm but found this impossible. When he got as far as the forward end of the main deck, he saw all the decks hidden in smoke. The time was now approximately noon.

By 12.30 the situation was becoming hopeless; the panelling of the main stairway between B and R deck was ablaze and people were fighting fires all over the ship. The shore-based fire fighting party came to assist after some of the fires had been abandoned by the crew as being out of control. The original fire discovered by the cabin boys had been fought for an hour and a quarter and eventually extinguished. Yet, on the moment of this triumph, nearly eighty yards aft and more than two hundred yards forward of this hard won battle and totally unconnected with it, there were more raging fires. In total there had been outbreaks in nine separate locations that made the ship beyond saving!

What made the episode so sinister was the fact that the Queen Elizabeth had been designed so that fire risks were cut down to an absolute minimum. The ship was fitted throughout with firescreen bulkheads, fire-screen doors and smokescreen doors. All electrical wiring was laid out so that any danger of fire through overloading or short-circuiting was obviated. Fire-proof paint was used in many places and the ship was equipped with its own fire station which was, in Cunard's day, constantly manned and under the control of the master-at-arms who was in direct communication with both the bridge and the engine room. On the walls of the fire station hung elaborate deck plans of the entire ship which showed the position of every fire alarm and showed the duty fireman which of them had been rung if fire broke out. In addition, there was a smoke indicator

***The liner's final claim to fame was as the ficticious location of the British Secret Service headquarters in a James Bond film (Cobwebs collection)***

which was not only an instant detector of fire, but which also revealed the exact location. From all holds, cargo spaces, baggage rooms and stores, smoke detecting pipes led into the fire station where each ended with a small funnel under continuous watch of a photo electric cell. If smoke was drawn up any one of the pipes, it actuated the cell which lit the smoke as it passed out of the tiny funnel. Using this, the duty fireman could see at a glance not only whether fire had broken out, but also exactly where it had happened. He also had under his control a $CO_2$ gas apparatus and could flood an affected area with extinguishing materials immediately the indicator revealed the presence of fire.

The liner also featured a comprehensive self-actuating sprinkler system which could both detect and extinguish fire in the passenger quarters. Added to this there were normal water-main supply systems with various fire fighting points. By means of an appropriate indicator panel the bridge could be instantly informed of fire and should have been able, using the comprehensive communications system, to co-ordinate necessary measures. The circumstances were extraordinary. The liner had enjoyed an incredibly good fire safety record throughout her career and now, with the new conversion almost complete, she should have been better than ever. Many of the original Cunard crew were amazed that the ship could burn so quickly and so completely, unless the blaze had been deliberately started in several key areas of the ship at the same time. Commodore Marr was asked for his opinions in press and television interviews at the time and he expressed similar opinions to those above. He even received a telephone call from one of Hong Kong's leading newspapers asking for clarification of his comments. He simply replied that he knew the ship very well and mentioned that he had suffered at the hands of an arsonist on board the Carinthia in Montreal.

Unfortunately the fire destroyed any evidence and no official enquiry ever really established exactly what happened. For a whole day and night the Hong Kong firemen attempted to control the blaze, pumping millions of gallons of water into the ship. Then, when she could take no more, she rolled over on to the harbour bottom and lay burnt-out and half-submerged to become a tourist attraction as junks and launches ferried passengers close to her. The marine court of enquiry brought a verdict of probable arson but no-one was ever charged. The brand new replicas of the Chinese Great Hall of the Sages and the Tang Emperor's Moon Palace, together with the Peacock Lounge that had been constructed on board were never seen. Perhaps it was best that way, with the ship being remembered as the largest passenger liner in the world. Commodore Marr said that the ship had earned her Viking's funeral and if there was a heaven for ships the Queen Elizabeth would undoubtedly be there.

# X The Royal Replacement

On July 4, 1965, the first section of the QE2's keel was laid at the Clydebank shipyards, marking the 125th Anniversary of the maiden voyage of the first Cunarder, the Britannia, in 1840.

The responsibility for the structural design of the QE2 was entrusted to Dan Wallace, chief Naval architect of the Cunard Line. Wallace's work on the ship had begun back in 1954 when Cunard were considering a successor to the Queen Mary. In fact, the Mary was the first ship on which Wallace worked when he was an employee at John Brown's Yard. He joined Cunard in 1951 as assistant naval architect and took over from Bob Wood in April 1964. The ultimate success of the new liner would depend on its ability to function as a passenger carrying machine, an operation handed to Tom Kameen, who was made director of new construction and engineering research with Cunard. Kameen had joined in 1936, going to sea as an engineer officer. After the war he became assistant superintendent engineer with Cunard, being appointed to technical director in 1963.

The QE2 was being built on a modular system, in that one section of the ship and its fittings were completed before work moved onto the next, with Cunard utilizing a computer to keep a close check on exactly what was being achieved on a daily basis. However, it wasn't programmed to detect the losses of large quantities of furnishings, bathroom fittings and electrical equipment which were systematically being stripped out of the ship under cover of darkness. The workers maintained that the more you stole from the ship that you were building, then the longer it would take to finish the job, and hence, the longer you were employed. Captain Arnott in his book "Captain of the Queen" tells a tale of the police in 1968 searching the home of one electrician who was working on the ship at the time. Apparently, he was found to have taken thirty yards of carpet, two chests of drawers, a wall cabinet, three bookcases, three lounge stools, four settee backs, one toilet seat, five lamp shades, one bulkhead lamp, one shower valve, one drilling brace, three strip lighting units, an electric radiator, eight electric bulbs, 180 feet of fibreglass, four wooden gratings, four curtain rails, five sheets of plastic, two buckets, eight gallons of paint, a roll of wire netting, six teacups and saucers, six side plates, six cereal plates, three cushions, five curtains, two sheets, a blanket, a canvas tarpaulin, five flourescent tubes, 350 feet of electric cable and 216 yards of sellotape!

At the time of the ship's construction there was a thriving black market around Glasgow for anything that bore an exclusive QE2 design. The story goes that formica sheets could be stolen and sold for ten shillings, delivered to your door. And the bright orange, green and red paint used in the engine-room could be retailed at £1 per gallon, once again including delivery. Apparently on one

***Although not quite as long as the Queen Elizabeth that she replaced, the QE2 still provided an almost never ending perspective along her decks (Author photo)***

Monday morning, two fully-equipped new lifeboats were delivered, by the next day they were stripped of everything that would move. The police were unwilling to clamp down too hard on the "squirreling" as it was known, maintaining that their appearance at the yard would cause too much trouble and probably result in stoppages far more expensive than the cost of replacing the stolen items.

The QE2 was to be the ultimate £30 million floating holiday resort, able to follow the sun around the world. She was planned at under 70,000 tons with other vital statistics such as her 963 foot length, 32½ foot draught and 105 foot breadth designed to allow her to negotiate the Panama canal. She would also be able to use the Suez canal and visit ports that had been out of bounds to the other Queens due to their deep draughts.

Compared with the Queen Elizabeth where each passenger had an average of 39.5 square feet of enclosed public space and 47.75 square feet of sheltered open deck space, on the QE2, each passenger would, on the maiden voyage (subsequent changes altered this) have approximately 53.7 square feet and 72.6 square feet respectively and be able to enjoy 6,000 yards of deck, a departure from the limited outdoor space provided on the earlier Queens. Overall, the figures would mean total increases for each passenger of over 52%. A significant reason for this was the inclusion of an extra thirteenth deck, made possible by the use of aluminium in the building of the ship's superstructure. The QE2 would be 14 feet higher than the Queen Elizabeth, but narrower by 13 feet. All the public rooms aboard the ship were to be constructed within the aluminium superstructure above main deck level which would provide a far greater amount of window space than that carried on her sister ships. To further provide for cruising, four pools were planned – two internal and two external.

***The funnel design was a radical departure from that employed on earlier Cunarders – when the ship first went into service, it wasn't even displaying these Cunard colours, instead it was a monochrome black and white (Cobwebs collection)***

Stabilizers, the fitting of which had proved so successful on the earlier royal pair, were also employed on the new liner and were said to be able to "limit rolling down to a mere three degrees".

The funnel was a radical departure from all the others Cunarders and developed by the Cunard technical department after lengthy testing in the wind tunnel at the National Physical Laboratory at Teddington, Middlesex. Numerous models were constructed and tried before the final design was approved, resulting in the most technically advanced smokestack ever to be fitted to a passenger vessel. The original structure, which has since been altered, comprised a small diameter smokestack, large air outlet vent and a wind scoop mounted on a fan house which covered the air intake.

The main driving machinery of the QE2 originally consisted of two sets of Brown-Pametrada steam turbines built by John Brown Engineering. The design of the turbines and boilers was arranged so that, if required, the machinery could operate at a temperature of 1000 degrees F. Another achievement was in the size of the electrical generating plant – the turbo-alternators being the largest ever installed in a merchant ship at the time. The 3,300 volt system terminated in a number of large transformers which provided current at 415 volts and also 240 volts to power all of the various motor drives and supply electricity to the services throughout the cabins and public rooms. Four main propellers were originally manufactured for the QE2, although only two were in use at any one time. All four were supplied by Stone Manganese Marine Ltd., and built to the firm's Meridian design in Superston Seventy alloy, weighing 31.75 tons. Each had six blades of 19 feet with a pitch of 21.65 feet and a developed area of 254 square feet. The same company made the two bow thrust units of Stone KaMeWa design. These were fitted one behind the other in the forepeak, with each unit capable of a lateral thrust of up to 11 tons. Their purpose being to facilitate manoeuvring of the ship in a confined space, consequently enabling fewer tugs to be required for berthing operations.

The mast was the last part of the vessel to leave the drawing board. In the completed structure there were many purposes being served and before the final design was agreed upon, fifteen different models were produced. At the top of the mast was a satellite navigation aerial, two eleven foot radar scanners, two navigation lights, two groups of code lamps and two whistles, one of which was operated by compressed air, the other by electricity. There were also two light detectors which controlled the illumination in the main restaurant, together with two loud hailers plus signal and courtesy flag halyards. The mast also acted as a duct for carrying off fumes from the galleys.

The QE2 was to have 687 rooms in common accommodation and each of these would be equipped with a bath or shower. This offered a total of 1,441 berths. In addition to this there were 291 deluxe appointed rooms with 46 of these being

designated as luxury suites. Ship-to-shore transport, which was still essential for many of the proposed stop-overs, was taken care of by totally enclosed motor cruisers with big windows and coach type tops that could carry eighty people per trip. As well as this there would be 12, thirty-six foot motor lifeboats and two water-jet propelled emergency sea boats together with 62 inflatable rafts each capable of saving the lives of 25 people.

The bridge was becoming hi-tech and the QE2 was going to be the first merchant ship to feature a computer that could handle data logging, alarm scanning, machinery control, prediction of fresh water needs, weather implications and overall control of food stocks.

On September 20, 1967, the ship was ready for launching and Her Majesty the Queen performed the ceremony.

After fitting-out was completed, the QE2 embarked on the traditional measured mile test which resulted in her return to dock for a further

***Ship to shore transport was taken care of with totally enclosed motor cruisers (Author photo)***

thirteen days whilst a few problems were ironed out. This forced the cancellation of a press cruise, and meant that by the time the Queen Elizabeth 2 was ready she really should have been sailing on her first money-making cruise for Cunard. The majority of the seagoing population were pleased with the new ship, however there were some traditionalists who complained about the bulbous bow area beneath the waterline. They maintained that there should be a foaming bow wave when the ship was travelling at speed! The new design had rendered this obsolete to reduce turbulence.

When the 1,000 or so crew embarked, they

***The QE2 made front page headlines when she was launched on September 20 1967 (Author photo)***

# Daily Mirror

*Just christened..and the new Queen Elizabeth II is VERY slow to take the plunge*

4d. Thursday, September 21, 1967 * * * No. 19,826

# LAUNCH OF THE LAZY LIZZIE

**BEAUTIFUL!** *The Queen and the Duke of Edinburgh are caught up in a great wave of delight as the newly-named Queen Elizabeth II, towering above them goes down to the Clyde. "She's beautiful!," the Queen said.*

## 70 seconds..and nothing happens

*By Mirror Reporter*

SHE'S launched... but for seventy almost agonising seconds yesterday it looked as if the newly-christened liner Queen Elizabeth II was refusing to take the plunge.

Even the Queen looked a bit anxious after she had pressed a button to release the launching gear at John Brown's shipyard on the Clyde.

It looked a cliffhanger, too, to millions watching on TV—but Cunard chiefs remained buoyant and said afterwards that there was nothing really unusual about the new liner's seeming reluctance.

Everything had gone smoothly enough when the Queen cut a ribbon to smash a bottle of champagne on the 58,000-ton liner's bows.

Then came the seventy seconds when—to inexpert eyes, at any rate—the Queen Elizabeth II didn't seem to budge.

Workmen high up on her deck leaned and shouted: "Give us a shove!"

Shipyard director George Parker joined in the spirit of the request.

Bowler-hatted, he sprang to the bows and gave the liner a shove. And jubilantly waved his bowler when, by a coincidence, she began to move.

In a little over two minutes after the Queen had said "May God bless her and all who sail in her," the new Elizabeth had slid smoothly into the Clyde.

*The Man who Gave Her a Push —See Centre Pages.*

found themselves with five recreation rooms and four crew restaurants. With the full contingent of manpower at last on board, the liner was ready for its somewhat belated voyage down to Southampton which was to become her home port. During the two day voyage south, workers were still completing small tasks that still hadn't been finished, and a ferry boat was hired to house the Clydesiders as they toiled against time. Cunard weren't taking any chances that more "souvenirs" would go missing!

Of equal importance to the overall structural design of the ship was the interior design work which featured a complete departure from the earlier Queens. The co-ordination of the many designs and ideas involved was divided between two people, Dennis Lennon and James Gardner. Lennon was chosen to co-ordinate the efforts of ten top interior designers, with their object being to "create a unified interior for the ship, complimenting its character with ideas that would reflect the best in contemporary design and manufacture". Lennon's own team of designers were responsible for the restaurants on board, many of the cabins, the cocktail bars, a library and a swimming pool as well as all entrances, alleyways and staircases.

In the past, Lennon had been commissioned to work on the Cumberland Hotel in London, 32 London steak-houses for J. Lyons and a chain of shops for Jaeger. He had also been called in to advise in the re-decoration of the auditorium of the Rome Opera House, plus a housing scheme of 35 acres in Hampstead for the council. After the QE2, he began working on Piccadilly Circus redevelopment scheme.

James Gardner had been given the job of sorting out the exterior aesthetics of the ship. His task required him to "bring unity and order to the result of functional engineering". His previous commissions included the design co-ordination of the 1951 South Bank exhibition, and as chief designer of the festival gardens at Battersea and also the British Pavilion at the Expo '67 in Montreal. His work had ranged from the design of jewellery to hovercraft.

Their resultant work was very striking and featured many contemporary construction materials such as tubular steel and formica. Whether the desired result had been achieved was a matter for speculation, with many older passengers aghast at the appearance of the new Cunarder. When the ship first docked at Southampton and took on passengers for her maiden voyage, they would have been greeted with public rooms positioned on the top 5 decks of the 13 on the ship. Those below being devoted almost exclusively to accommodation. The Midships Lobby on two deck, is where we come aboard. Dennis Lennon and partners were responsible for this lobby. It is circular with a sunken seating area in the centre where people can meet friends. The carpets are navy, walls are lined with navy hide and the sofas in the seating well are covered in green leather. There is an enquiry desk and round glass coffee tables designed by William Plunkett. The silvered fibreglass ceiling flows to the outer walls in concentric circles like the pattern made by a stone dropped into a pool of still water. A centre column is covered in shiny white fibreglass with white ribs emanating from this across the mirror finish of the ceiling. Cedar veneered passageways lead off to the cabins and to the lifts and stairs from which you can ascend to the signal deck, the highest level on the ship which features an observation platform.

The next deck down is the sports deck which, apart from having provision for all the usual shipboard games, also has a large area devoted to children. When design plans were being made, Dennis Lennon suggested to Sir Hugh Casson, Head of Interior Design at the Royal College of Art, that his students should work on this room and on the coffee shop and juke box on the boat deck. The students were asked to submit ideas, and on the basis of these, two students were chosen, Elizabeth Beloe and Tony Heaton, to go ahead with the work. The children's room with a sand-coloured floor inset with orange and yellow hopscotch was their first idea, followed by a shallow pool for wet activities, ranges of storage cupboards with sliding doors covered in blackboard and striped formica and also chequer board tables, whose tops could be removed to reveal fibreglass trays. In addition they designed stools which doubled as building blocks, and divided the room into different areas using curved fibreglass screens that were white on one side and orange on the other.

One deck down is a coffee shop which can be turned into a disco. It features curved red vinyl-covered chairs grouped in booths around brown formica-topped with a black perimeter line. In the main area of the room the walls and doors are lined with formica striped in bright colours. The floor is carpeted in black with a strip of mirror-bright stainless steel forming the skirting board and also a dado at head level. To one side leading aft is a raised gallery that has booths with more tables looking out to sea, and waist high walls with curving red upholstered rails. One end of this area is set aside for pin tables and a juke box together with a 100 foot mural by Tim Sarson depicting moving figures separated by tall strips of distorted mirror.

Forward of this is the 736 club, named after the shipyard number by which the QE2 was known prior to her launching. This room was entrusted to architects Stefan Buzas and Alan Irvine. By the use of wood veneers they aimed at a ship-like quality. Passing through the double doors between two troughs of green plants near the bandstand are bulkheads lined with Indian laurel veneer together with tan-coloured leather upholstery in grouped seating areas on a carpet of rich blue/green. There are two banks of chairs, one in alcoves around the outside of the room and another grouped around the lowered dance floor with its gold leaf ceiling. Satin nickel brackets consisting of three ship's lens lamps are used for lighting. These are mounted on timber veneered columns around the dance floor and allow a disco atmosphere to be created in the room when necessary.

The London Gallery on the boat deck was designed by the same pair of architects and is lined with beige and brown formica on a dark blue carpet. Inboard are showcases for the display of small objects, and along the outboard wall screens made of cream "canotex" clip into the floor at intervals to make a variety of display arrangements for paintings and exhibitions.

The balcony of the theatre lies between this London Gallery and a teenage arcade, then further on are arcades of shops down both sides of the ship. The same navy blue carpet is used, with bulkheads lined with two shades of blue formica. Beyond these shopping arcades are doors to the top level of the double room. This, designed by John Bannenberg is one of the largest and most dramatic rooms in the ship. It covers 20,000 square feet and has seating for 800. Furnishing is in various shades of scarlet through to plum. From the upper gallery a stainless-steel curved staircase with treads five feet wide sweeps down into the lower room. Its sepia tinted balustrade with scarlet handrail continues around the upper level. All the furniture is by William Plunkett and is in plum leather, puce-suede and scarlet-tweed. A bold herring-bone patterned carpet, also designed by Bannenberg, incorporates all these colours, achieving a measure of harmony with the anodised aluminium and textured formica walls. There are two bars in the double room, one at the upper level, and one in the lower room which also serves the deck space beyond from where passengers can look down on to the open air swimming pool below. There is a circular bandstand on the lower level similar to two stacked pennies – the bottom one slides out to provide a bigger stage if required.

Further forward on the upper deck is the tour office designed by Gaby Schrieber. It has a tan carpet, chairs upholstered in caramel suede and cyclamen wool, and panels of tangerine wool on the aluminium bulkheads. Storage cupboards are faced in rosewood and the desks can be pushed together when the room is used for conferences. Two more rooms, both designed by Dennis Lennon, are also on this deck. The first, on the port side, is the upper deck library. The second is to starboard and called the theatre bar. The library features a thick-ribbed beige carpet, blue leather-lined cases for the books with latticed metal screens to keep them in place. Seating is in large sofas with shelves along their backs to support reading lamps. The centre of the room is taken up with a circular rosewood leather-topped table around which are placed other deep chairs in pale blue tweed. To complete the decor, stripy curtains by Conran are used plus blinds that can be pulled down to ward off the sun's glare.

The theatre bar has the same carpeting but a much less restrained atmosphere. The facing wall is bright red fibreglass in an egg box pattern with a nearby grand piano to colour match. The red scheme continues with the long sofas which are joined by shiny metal chairs with red tweed cushions against curtains of red and orange. Low tables, designed by William Plunkett, are also provided which all combine to make the room extremely lively to say the least.

The theatre itself leads off from this bar and is another of Gaby Schrieber's contributions. It provides seating for over 500 and was designed to fulfil four uses, theatre, cinema, conference room and, on Sundays, a church. Lighting has been

implemented to assist in these transformations and seats are covered in bright plum/mauve striped wool by Bernat Klien. They are equipped with removable flap-down trays for conferences and have pockets to take short-wave receivers for simultaneous translations. The ceiling of this multi-purpose room is of pre-formed fibreglass panelling whilst the rear wall is faced with slatted acoustic materials.

Between the Theatre Bar and Britannia restaurant is a promenade area with chairs and small tables which acts as an ante-room to the restaurant itself. Designed by Dennis Lennon, the Britannia has seating for 815 people with panoramic views across the sea. The room takes up the entire width of the ship and employs a patriotic red, white and blue colour scheme. White fibreglass bulkheads, blue tweed banquettes and red handrails along the windows combine here with white tablecloths banded with red – and red table napkins banded with white. The carpet has a two-tone blue pattern whilst blinds feature a flower pattern in blue and white. The ceiling is made from cedar veneer boarding with downlighter spotlights recessed into it above each of the tables. On the same theme, there is indirect lighting from behind screens and polished brass louvres mounted on the bulkheads. Decorations include a Britannia figurehead carved in Quebec yellow pine by Cornish sculptor Charles Moore. There are also two woodens ship's moulds at the aft end of the room, and in the centre are models of two early Cunard vessels; the Britannia and the Persia.

Nearby on the same deck is the Look Out. This is a two-level room with a view across the bows. It was designed by Crosby/Fletcher/Forbes, who were also responsible for the graphics throughout the ship. Bulkheads here are faced in Cedar of Lebanon and there is an olive green carpet and moulded fibreglass chairs upholstered in black cirrus. White plastic-topped tables by Arkana are trimmed with bronze aluminium which complement the brown roller blinds. Special wooden shutters have been fitted to prevent light from this area interfering with the ship's navigation at night. The main feature is the aft wall behind the bar, made up of multi-faceted stainless-steel panels interspersed with bronze anodised-aluminium mullions. It was produced from an idea by Theo Crosby by artist Gillian Wise and makes the whole room appear larger. Another interesting device is a microfilm reader which shows charts of the areas into which the ship will travel and is available for use by the passengers. Music is provided for by another bright red grand piano.

***John Bannenberg's 20,000 square foot original double room (Cobwebs collection)***

On the quarter deck below, the fore end of the ship is occupied by an enormous stainless steel main kitchen. Beyond this is the Columbia restaurant, again designed by Dennis Lennon. This is smaller than the Britannia but still extends the full width of the ship. It has been divided into smaller areas by using bronze-tinted glass screens. The carpet is brown to complement ochre leather wall-panels and pale apricot curtains by Tamesa. The ceilings and columns are faced with gold aluminium and the chairs, designed by Robert Heritage, have polished aluminium legs and are upholstered in dark brown leather. Tablecloths are changed in this room according to the time of day; for breakfast and lunch the centre tables are lemon, with pale beige for those around the perimeter, whilst at dinner, the centre tables change to pink. Special table lamps are used in the evening that consist of 2½ inch solid blocks of perspex on stainless steel bases. A 24 volt light source, with a reflector fitted into a column of the table beneath shines up through the table cloth and turns this sculptured perspex block into a glowing column. The light is refracted and dispersed from each face of the perspex which is held securely in position by four permanent magnets.

Two side-areas intended for private parties lead off from this room. They have yellow leather wall-panels and pale yellow curtains. Outside the main entrance is a tapestry by Helena Barynini Hernmark depicting the launching of the ship and just forward and discreetly inaccessible, as it can only be reached by a circular staircase from its own bar on the deck below, is the Grill Room. This is an exclusive 100 seat restaurant, utilizing the same perspex column lighting as the Columbia. The bulkheads are panelled in Bordeaux red leather and velvet with shiny metal trim. Banquettes are buttoned in a brighter shade of red and there are leather covered chairs by Mies van der Rohe. Silvery silk curtains have silver concertina blinds to match and lifesize statues by Janine Janet lit from above and below are poised at four points in the room representing the four elements, fire, earth, water and air. They are made entirely from materials of the sea such as shells, coral and mother-of-pearl.

The Midships bar on the quarter deck is aft of the Columbia restaurant on the starboard side. Again by Dennis Lennon, this acts as the ante-room for the nearby restaurant. Curved sofas and walls in rich green leather and mohair velvet are featured on a green carpet. William Plunkett chairs upholstered in even brighter green stand alongside the same designer's tinted glass tables whilst onion-shaped lamps shine down onto them. There are three white abstract paintings in the room by artist Richard Lin, together with a brass sphere showing the relationship between the planets and the earth. This was presented to Cunard by the Institute of London Underwriters.

The promenade area outside has standard white rubber flooring and magnolia formica bulkhead facings with Bertoia chairs. Green and white check blinds complement a dark green upholstery with more low-set lights, this time in cylindrical chrome fittings, ranged between troughs of plants.

The port side on the same deck includes the card room and the quarter deck library. The former is designed by John Bannenberg and is lined with panels of green suede and green baize with a brighter green outlining the entrances to the two small booths raised up on one side. The chairs are also upholstered in green suede and the six fixed rosewood centre-tables have green baize tops. The theme is maintained in the green and beige carpet design by John Crossley. The library next door is designed by Michael Inchbald who has used traditional finishes of wood and brass with bulkheads lined in wood veneer, and books stowed behind wooden roller shutters. There are chesterfield sofas upholstered in brown tweed, and chairs in bright green leather together with upright seating in brass and black leather. Brass is also used in the bound ship's chests which, fitted with black formica tops, are used as side tables on a textured bright green carpet.

***The Queen's room – as it looked on the ship's maiden voyage (Cobwebs collection)***

Further aft is the white and silver Queens Room by the same designer. To lengthen the appearance of the square area, fore and aft the walls have a sculptured walnut block effect built onto them interspersed with mirrors to lengthen the perspective. A slotted white ceiling with lighting behind gives a trellised effect and the structural columns are encased in inverted trumpets of white glass fibre. The chairs are made of the same material with natural hide upholstery and have bases of this trumpet shape in reverse. White lacquered sofas with flame tweed upholstery are grouped around the edge of the lower section of the room and instead of a rail marking the change in level, there is a low white lacquered ledge inset with plant troughs. Sliding glass walls between this room and the promenades have fine wool curtains in vertical random stripes of orange, white and honey and lemon. These colours are picked up on the scatter cushions and the carpet.

Finally, on the same deck is a conference centre and also the Q4 room designed by David Hicks. This is a nightclub which opens onto the swimming pool on the deck beyond. The walls are lined with panels of grey flannel in polished aluminium frames separated by strips of gold leaf. The carpet is in black, grey and red checks and translucent screens stand on it. These are made of perspex rods sandwiched between sheets of polarised glass, producing a rainbow of soft colours. Tablecloth changing also takes place in this room, where during the day, pink is used but swapped at night for black with grey stripes around the edge.

Cunard decided, once the interior was completely finished, it would be sensible to run a short shakedown cruise as a dress rehearsal for the real maiden voyage. It was operated with company personnel and their families playing the role of the fee-paying passengers, and thoroughly testing out each and every one of the ship's services, before she was finally accepted from the shipbuilders. The cruise went to West Africa and enabled the air conditioning system which had caused so much discomfort on the earlier Queens, to be tried out. It worked perfectly in the 90 degree temperatures and

***The new Cunarder takes to the oceans – over the years, her superstructure would undergo considerable change, especially forward of the funnel (Cobwebs collection)***

so the ship was handed over to Cunard. A few days later the QE2 finally left on her maiden voyage to New York. There were bands playing on the quayside, and large crowds of well-wishers as the ship nosed her way out into Southampton Water, passing tankers, yachts and tugs crammed with people shouting and cheering the ship.

The welcome in New York several days later was its traditional best with the whole harbour ablaze with coloured bunting, and the air filled with blasts from boats that crammed the harbour approaches. The New York fireboats provided a display of waterfalls with their powerful hoses and sightseeing helicopters buzzed the ship. Two R.A.F. Harrier jets hovered, one at each extremity of the bridge, where they stayed until the ship had entered harbour.

When the ship was safely tied up a party was held on board, with dancing to the George Haley Orchestra in the Double Room, the Applejacks in the Theatre Bar, the Canadian Edmund Hockridge singing show hits with the Basil Stutely Orchestra in the Queen's Room, Dougie Ward and his trio

***The OE2 continued the tradition of being a sophisticated means of luxury travel for the rich and famous (Author photo of Cobwebs collection)***

providing popular folk in the Q4 room, and if that wasn't enough, the Midships Bar featured George Feyer and his piano. The ship was complete – at least until the guests left and Cunard found that they were missing hundreds of condiment sets and linen table napkins. But this time the Clydeside workers couldn't be blamed!

The ship was populated by the world's rich and famous, and Captain Bob Arnott recounts an interesting story which shows how much the passengers respected the officers of the ship. Apparently he was sitting in the green velvet of the Midships bar sipping an after dinner whisky when Natalie Wood and her estranged husband, Robert Wagner came in. "What do you think, Bob," said Natalie, "about our getting together again? We're considering giving our marriage another go. Do you think we should?"

Apparently, Bob looked apprehensively at the nonchalant expression of Wagner, and worried that, if he gave the wrong answer, he might just get a punch on the nose. However, Wagner was nodding to Natalie's query, and inviting the advice. So Bob replied. "Well, you've got a lot going for you, and I'd say that by the way you're holding hands and adoring each other with your eyes, then it would be sheer cruelty to keep you apart."

Natalie smiled. "Oh thanks, Bob," she said. "I was hoping that you'd say something like that!" The couple walked away and had soon repaired their marriage, which continued until Natalie's tragic drowning in 1981.

However, for all the surface success, the early years of the QE2 weren't good ones for Cunard and they suffered considerable financial losses in the early seventies and were eventually forced into a takeover by Trafalgar House Group. The new owners' plan was to market the QE2 aggressively in every possible way. Trafalgar House didn't want the new Queen to go the way her sisters had gone and so within a few weeks of the takeover, a letter had been issued to hundreds of eminent and wealthy people inviting them to buy a trip on the ship. Many did, and in winter 1971, fifty per cent more people travelled on the ship than in 1970. A ship on the high seas is an easy target for pirates, even today, and a similar modern version of the swashbuckling tales can be told about the QE2 – a true story – which occured on May 17, 1972, at night in the Atlantic. It all started with a radio room incoming message: "Threat of explosion to destroy ship unless demand cash payment met. Explosives set on six separate decks. Authorities advise take all necessary precautions. Two accomplices may be on board. Monitor all cables and telephone messages."

At New York a few hours earlier, a strange call

***The ship went through several different colour schemes during her early years – note the few feet of black hull still visible at her bows during this repainting session (Cobwebs collection)***

had been taken from an extortionist demanding $350,000. If it wasn't paid he was threatening to blow the QE2 out of the sea! He reported that he had two accomplices that were journeying on the ship and were ready to die if the ransom went unpaid. An emergency meeting of Chiefs of Staff at the Ministry of Defence in London was held after Cunard requested assistance. The decision to send bomb disposal experts was taken by Admiral Sir Michael Pollock, Chief of Naval Staff and First Sea Lord, together with Air Chief Marshal Sir Denis Spotwood, Chief of Air Staff. Details of the parachute drop were worked out by the joint defence planning and operational staff and the Royal Marines and the Army were asked to each provide two top bomb disposal experts. Urgent phone calls were made to service units to get the four-man team together, while preparations for the 1,500 mile flight were made at the R.A.F. base at Lyneham in Wiltshire.

In London, Victor Matthew, chairman of Cunard, stated that "this is probably a con trick and a very clever one, but we cannot take any chances." Captain Law, master on the QE2 at the time, informed the passengers of the situation. The money was requested in 10 and 20 dollar bills and the company would be given instructions on how to hand it over in a second call. At a board meeting in London it was agreed to pay the ransom, and the money was subsequently put at the disposal of the FBI. The board meeting also discussed the mystery of how the two men on the QE2 expected to know when the money was paid. It was finally reasoned that in the circumstances, it wouldn't be too difficult for them to pick-up a radio signal from the American coast.

A former Scotland Yard man aboard the QE2 had been placed in charge of the security operation on the ship, and the crew had been given specific instructions from London on how the liner should be searched. Cunard officials explained that it was an impossible task to check every single item of baggage taken aboard, but maintained that one suitcase bomb would not have sufficient force to endanger the ship. However, they did carry out exhaustive searches but found nothing.

Meanwhile, a secret rendezvous was planned for the parachute drop. The four experts hit the water just 200 yards from the ship, climbed aboard and began searching, but they too found nothing. On Thursday, May 18, 1972, a letter arrived at the Cunard offices in New York telling them to take £350,000 to a designated phone booth. The money was duly taken and as it was being deposited, the phone in the booth rang and a voice ordered the ransom transferred to the washroom of a nearby cafe. The cash was left and the surroundings watched discreetly by the FBI, but no one collected the money and next day it was returned to Cunard.

A few years later, in July 1976, the liner was involved in another scare. The ship was heading out past Bishop Rock Lighthouse on to the Atlantic when she caught fire. The boiler-room was badly damaged and the liner was forced to return to Southampton unable to carry her passengers to New York. This resulted in extensive repairs followed by sea trials.

Like her royal sisters, the QE2 had her fair share of wealthy regulars. The story goes that one retired gold miner, Walter Gostyla, from Connecticut had made over 90 crossings on the ship by 1976 with the proceeds of an income from a lifelong investment in oil stocks.

Pets were welcomed on board and the new ship had kennels provided for animals up to about the size of an Alsatian, but not for a pack of eight massive Irish Wolfhounds that Captain Arnott saw being brought aboard at the start of one trip. There was no room for the animals, but because the two lady owners looked so sad, kind-hearted Bob arranged for the ship's carpenters to construct special kennels for the massive dogs which were then sited in the crew's cinema.

Travel on the QE2 wasn't cheap, and in 1977 it could cost up to £62,000 a head for the world cruise in the pampered luxury of the two top penthouse suites – the Queen Anne or the Trafalgar. However, most passengers made do with simpler staterooms with prices at a somewhat more realistic £4,000 and upwards. Considerable provisions were loaded on board for the world cruises, and some measure of the amounts required can be judged from the fact that in crossing the Atlantic alone, 12,000 gallons of milk was used up, a far cry from the fresh milk supplied by the Britannia's solitary cow.

The QE2 even had its own special whisky. Billed as the "world's most exclusive Scotch", it was 85 per cent proof and guaranteed to be at least 12 years old. The liquid came from the Duke of Argyll's Inverary Distillery, and soon the barmen on the

***Certificates were presented to passengers travelling on QE2 (Author photos of Cobwebs collection)***

***The QE2 even had its own special whisky (Author photo of Cobwebs collection)***

ship had come up with many exotic ideas for its use including QE2 coffee consisting of cream, coffee, brown sugar, creme de cacao, and, of course, the whisky! The chefs soon got in on the act too, keen not to be outdone, and produced Shrimp Clan Campbell, which featured seafood marinated in the new Scotch.

Over the years, the QE2 was modified both internally and externally. Perhaps the most radical of these early alterations was in 1978 when the ship was treated to some splendid new rooms whilst at the Bethlehem Steel Corporation's dry dock in New Jersey. During a seventeen-day overhaul which cost over £2.5 million, a pair of pre-assembled luxury penthouses which were to be called the Queen Mary and Queen Elizabeth Suites were fitted into place on the signal deck behind the bridge. They weighed fifteen tons each and were constructed from a framework of welded aluminium. The price that passengers would be charged for tenancy in one of the new bolt-on-boxes was about £1,000 per day. However, for that figure, they would receive the best and most luxurious accommodation on any ship afloat. The interior of these new staterooms featured a split level bedroom/sitting room which had a twelve foot suede sofa, plus twin bathrooms with gold plated fittings, and a lounge supplied with music centre, stereo radio and record player, with the whole environment lit by specially designed completely user-variable Italian lighting and the very best furnishing gathered from Europe and America. More of these staterooms followed in later years.

The restaurants underwent change too, with the 836 Britannia restaurant becoming a completely new dining room called Tables of the World with the area divided up into five separate eating sections, with each one based on national themes. The Londoner was a typical English eating establishment with suitable old prints on the walls, together with models of famous old Cunard ships. The Florentine sported a smart white tile floor as a perfect setting for the dark blue velvet chairs and Pucii silk hangings. There was a Spanish area known as the Flamenco which was adorned with Picasso drawings of bullfights. Then a sunny Paris garden formed a backcloth and set the scene for the French Parisienne sector, and finally the Oriental in the middle of the restaurant featured a glittering pagoda surrounded by a gold ceiling, silver walls, black carpeting, and authentic bamboo hanging lanterns. Due to these alterations, new kitchens were added, as well as games rooms for the teenagers. Staterooms for 300 passengers were also refurbished, giving the whole of the ship an attractive new look. But the biggest conversion of all was still almost a decade away.

***The ship was treated to some splendid new rooms in 1978. They can be seen here forward of the funnel (Cobwebs collection)***

# XI

# The QE2: War Service

As the QE2 approached the English coast in May 1982 on route from Philadelphia, a B.B.C. news broadcast gave out the message that the ship had been requisitioned by the government to help out with Britain's disagreement with Argentina over the Falkland Islands. Although it had been half-expected, it was the first that Captain Jackson knew about the call-up. Confirmation followed just after midnight on May 4, as the ship berthed at Southampton, where the liner was immediately made available for war service. She would act as a troop ship for the Task Force that had been sent to repossess the Falkland Islands. The QE2 was to be in a similar situation to that which her sisters had experienced.

Conversion work began the following morning and decisions were made to slice off the upper deck at the stern in line with the club lido bar, together with the superstructure right down to quarterdeck level. This area could then provide a large landing pad site and service area for helicopters. Meanwhile up forward, the quarterdeck was being extended towards the bow right over the capstans so that another landing pad could be created there. Both of these had already been fabricated in record time by nearby ship repairers Vosper-Thornycroft, and while these were being fitted, interior items were removed from the ship and stored in Pickford's spacious Southampton warehouse. As soon as these items were clear of the ship, carpenters came on board and covered the corridors and all the carpeted interior decks with protective hardboard panels which were stuck in position with thick black tape. On the floor outside each cabin, in large letters, was printed the names of new inhabitants – eager young soldiers, some of which never returned.

In the double room where cabaret was normally the order of the day for cruise passengers seated in considerable luxury, there was an austere air created by the lines of plain trestle tables and chairs. In the war zone, this would provide troops with an area where they could relax by playing cards and drinking canned beer sold from the Naafi shop installed on the upper level of the two deck high room. This was normally the exclusive shopping arcade feature; most of the soldiers didn't have any requirement for perfume or exclusive fashions anyhow.

The ship's large cinema was rigged up for mass briefings and because there would be twice the normal passenger complement, public rooms such as the casino became dormitories, stripped bare of their glitter and glamour. Officers would eat in the Queens Grill, NCO's in the Princess Grill, with the Columbia and Tables of the World restaurants being converted into troop cafeterias. Other alterations included an independent radio room constructed behind the bridge, and also the laying of refuelling pipes from the starboard baggage entrance on two deck to the tanks six decks below.

***The quarterdeck was extended over the capstans so that another landing pad could be created there (Peter Boyd-Smith photo)***

Mid-ocean refuelling was essential for the QE2 to be able to make the trip down to the Falklands. Around this time, the news came through that HMS Sheffield had been hit by an Exocet missile and sustained heavy casualties. This had the general effect of strengthening resolve as the conversion came to an end.

Many tons of stores and equipment were loaded onto the liner including considerable quantities of extra life jackets and safety appliances. Ammunition was stored in number one hold and also in containers on the sports deck. Larger items or anything that could be required quickly, such as Landrovers, trailers, helicopter spares, fuel and emergency rations, was stored above. With sailing time arranged, Cunard asked for volunteers to man the ship. Around 650 were chosen out of over 1000 who offered. Although the trip was predominantly a masculine exercise, the crew did include 33 volunteer stewardesses.

After eight days of intense preparation, the QE2 was ready to go to war. John Nott, the Defence Minister, spent half an hour on board after the troops had embarked and emerged to report that "there was tremendous spirit on board," and added

SOUTHERN EVENING ECHO

Southampton — 85th year — No. 29831

Wednesday, May 12, 1982

FALKLAND ISLANDS COLOUR SPECIAL

# DUTY CALLS THE QE2

## PREPARING TO JOIN THE TASK FORCE

The QE2 in Southampton, preparing to sail for the Falklands.

# ON HER MAJESTY'S SERVICE

## LUXURY-CLASS TROOPSHIP

**GREAT LINERS have a habit of making history**

The Queen Mary's maiden voyage . . . the Queen Elizabeth's last — these were truly historic moments both for the world and Southampton, which has for so long been Britain's premier liner port.

Now we have Britain's largest and most prestigious passenger ship, a vessel that has always had the closest links with our city, preparing like so many of her predecessors to ferry 3,000 troops to a war zone.

Over the past week, the 67,000-ton cream of Britain's merchant marine has been transformed with breathtaking speed into a clinical instrument of war.

The change has proved to a new generation the amazing versatility of these elegant vessels. But it would not have been possible without the skill and dedication of local shipyard workers.

No one who has stood on the quayside at the Cunarder's berth in the Eastern Docks over the last few days can have failed to notice hundreds of people working extraordinarily hard in the face of a common call.

The staff of Vosper Shiprepairers and Vosper Thornycroft have slaved virtually night and day to fit three helicopter pads and make the ship ready for war.

Most of the luxury fittings have been stripped out and boards have been laid on her plush carpet to protect it from heavy army boots.

The operation has gone ahead with speed and efficiency and one ship electrician said: "The spirit of goodwill is amazing, with everyone throwing their weight behind the work that has to be done."

The phlegmatic Cunard managers, on hearing of the QE2's requisitioning while enjoying their Bank Holiday, threw themselves into a truly awe-inspiring planning operation, as they contacted passengers whose bookings had to be cancelled.

As the QE2 sails for the Falklands, the people of Hampshire can truly say a little piece of them is sailing with her.

MORE COLOUR PICTURES OF THE WORLD'S GREATEST LINER: BACK PAGE

***The third member of Cunard's royal trio was called up (Author photo)***

"I pray and hope for a peaceful solution, but if they have to fight they will aquit themselves in the great traditions of the British Army. But we in the government will do our best to see that this is not necessary." There were also words of praise for the soldiers from the Chief of General Staff, General Sir Edwin Bramall, who described the troops as having "great determination and confidence."

Cameras, binoculars, flags and handkerchiefs combined along Southampton's Weston Shore with ceremonial bands at the quayside to give the QE2 a colourful moving send-off. Helicopters circled overhead and made low level runs across the cheering crowds on the shoreline. There were banners too – one large white and one summed up the mood of the nation, reading 'Don't take no Argie-bargie". The QE2 sailed down Southampton Water to a piper playing "Scotland the Brave" with approximately 3,000 men of the Fifth Infantry Brigade, comprising of units of the Scots Guards, the Welsh Guards, and the Gurkha Rifles together with other Naval personnel and the Cunard crew. The 5th Brigade had been previously organized into a quick reaction force constantly prepared to move anywhere in the world outside the NATO theatre at just seven day's notice. They were sailing at the peak of readiness and battle fitness after having completed a tough exercise in the Welsh mountains, an area picked specially as it was deemed similar to the countryside of the Falkland Islands, "cold, wet and windy", as one officer described it. With the three infantry battalions there were also air defence,

***The converted QE2 sails to war (Peter Boyd-Smith photo)***

artillery, air support and logistic back-up troops who travelled as a complete brigade to the South Atlantic. In normal circumstances these would be split into combat teams and battle groups, each with its own specialized support depending on the role that they were undertaking, for the Falklands it was different.

Two support ferries, the Baltic and the Nordic had sailed a few days previously loaded with much of the equipment required by the Falklands garrison. A flight of Gazelle and three scout helicopters had been included in their contingent together with thousands of tons of other essential equipment.

The first task at sea was maintenance on a boiler, which was carried out shortly after sailing whilst the ship anchored off the Isle of Wight. With this back into operation, the QE2 could rely on full power for her voyage. Survival lectures and boat drills were held daily, together with exercise routines. It was vital to ensure that the refuelling system which had been installed was operating correctly, and so tests were made in the English Channel with a Royal Fleet Auxiliary tanker, Grey Rover. The QE2's fuelling port had been extended up from 5 deck to 2 deck and refuelling was effected by first running a messenger line across to link the two ships, which was then run through the 2 deck baggage room on the port side. The operation was hard work and a team of over one hundred crew were needed to haul the fuel hose. A token one ton was pumped successfully and the system verified as fully operational. The helicopter handling was also tested when two soldiers were transferred from the ship to shore, one with an appendicitis and the other with an injured foot.

The QE2 headed south, keeping clear of the main shipping lanes on a 3,000 mile voyage towards Freetown, Sierra Leone. Reports came through that some of the Soviet communications spy satellites were searching for the liner, and this significantly increased anxiety on cloudless days. By May 15, firing practice was being carried out over the bow and stern areas and it is said that there is still one white-painted stanchion on the fo'c'sle head that still has a bullet hole in it.

Many of the troops were in training around the ship – their heavy boots making the caulking fall out of many of the external teak decks. Added to this there was several hours flying practice for the Sea King crews each day, extremely important in view of the fact that most of the pilots had never flown on or off a merchant ship before. The most difficult landing spot soon became obvious, and none of the pilots liked the number one position fore of the bridge. It was made worse by the air currents which hit the liner and were then deflected upwards and sideways. The secret was apparently to try to consider the ship as a solid landing pad, match speed with her, maintain the position and then land safely – an extremely difficult manoeuvre.

The QE2 reached Sierra Leone after six days and 1,867 tons of extra fuel was taken on board, together with additional water and supplies. This enabled the liner to continue to the Falklands without need for further refuelling, and after slipping unnoticed out of the port, Captain Jackson headed for Ascension Island. The principal job now was completely to black-out the ship. Black paint was avoided where possible in favour of black garbage bags. The job took three days and was checked during night time helicopter flights in one of the two Sea King helicopters that were carried on board. The only problem with the bin-bag blackout was that, in the heat of the tropics, the bags crinkled up and the windows created a greenhouse effect which stretched the ship's air conditioning to the limit. Once again, the troops of forty years ago travelling on the other Queens were remembered, and the QE2's contingent realising how well off they were in comparison. This latter day army wasn't crammed like sardines into a hot hull suffering from deaths on account of heat exhaustion. In fact, there was a compulsory cool-off in the temporary swimming pool erected on the bow for the traditional initiation of troops who were crossing the equator for the first time.

Ascension Island was still a day and a half away when the ship was sighted by a Russian trawler known to be a surveillance vessel. It was the first setback of the voyage, and considered dangerous at the time. However, the original course was maintained and a rendezvous made with HMS Dumbarton Castle. This vessel, which usually acted as a Royal Navy North Sea oil rig protection ship, was equipped with helicopter landing facilities, and so the opportunity was taken to load stores and men from the Naval ship to the QE2. Next day, Friday May 21, General Moore, Commander of Land Forces landed on the QE2 and discussed the transfer

***None of the pilots liked the number one position fore of the bridge (Robin Davies photo)***

of the liner's troop contingent, whilst helicopters brought 200 tons of stores and 10 tons of mail on board for distribution.

On May 23, a Sunday, the ship headed south for the last leg of the voyage. The radar was switched off and the ship silenced. Round-the-clock lookouts were posted and all watertight doors closed. News was coming in of Argentine hits on several ships including Cunard's container vessel Atlantic Conveyor. As an effort to afford some protection, Browning machine guns were installed on the bridge wings and Blow Pipe air defence

***Heavy machine guns were positioned on the bridge wings (Robin Davies photo)***

missiles were set-up, with this forming the QE2's only armaments.

By noon on May 26, the ship was in position with the weather falling fast to below zero. The familiar zig-zagging that had been so successful with the Queen Mary and Queen Elizabeth in the second world war was employed. Even in the freezing conditions, the troops continued their relentless training. That night, the weather deteriorated to such an extent that icebergs became a very real danger, and the ship had to weave between the giant glaciers. This necessitated the switching on of the radar, even though it could give away the ship's position to the enemy. The radar picked up over one hundred bergs – each of which could easily sink the Queen, with some of the larger ones estimated at several million tons. Captain Jackson took charge on the bridge: his expert seamanship combined with a smattering of good luck avoided any incident even though visibility was often less than a mile. There was to be no "Titanic".

Top military officers left the QE2 at noon on May 27 to discuss further plans in HMS Antrim. Before doing so, Brigadier Wilson wrote the following message which was later published in the ship's own newspaper, the 5th Infantry Brigade/QE2 News. "Very shortly we shall all transfer to other ships off South Georgia and start on the last phase of our move to the Falkland Islands. It looks as if the brigade will be there about the 1st June, that is early next week. Once there, we shall join 3 Commando Brigade. We shall sort ourselves out and then start joint operations to recapture the islands.

Orders will be given out on landing. It is too early yet to issue a detailed plan, for it would be bound to change over the course of the next 5 days.

This is the final issue of this newspaper, and to the master and ship's company I would say 'thank you' for the way you have looked after us on this voyage. We have come to know you well, we admire you, and we shall always be proud to say that we sailed with you in your magnificent ship.

To the brigade, I would simply say this: 'We shall start earning our pay as a team shortly; and we are in this game to win!'"

The Queen Elizabeth 2 anchored off at Cumberland Bay, the Whaling Station at Grytviken, some 200 miles from the Falklands, meeting the P & O line's Canberra liner, the North Sea Ferry, Norland, and HMS Endurance together with several trawlers converted to minesweepers. Soon the troops were disembarking in the adverse weather conditions, and survivors from HMS Ardent, Coventry and Antelope which had been attacked by the Argentines were transferred to the QE2. During the final disembarkation, news came through that a British tanker, the British Wye, was under attack 400 miles North. This was worrying as it proved that the QE2 was also in range while lying in Cumberland Bay. For this reason, the ship was moved out as even before the off-loading of stores was completed.

The ship increased speed to eighteen knots and headed back into the treacherous icefield in the hope that this would make it more difficult for the Argentinians to spot her. The fuel situation was becoming critical as several attempts at refuelling had been unavoidably postponed due to bad weather: This resulted in the QE2 being down to just 1,000 tons – enough to provide only 1½ days sailing at full power. However, after a very difficult 12½ hour refuel, the ship eventually managed to take on 3,834 tons. Captain Peter Jackson called this the "absolute limit for that kind of tricky operation."

Essential lifeboat drills were carried out, but some of the survivors that the QE2 was now carrying who had seen their aluminium ships catch fire so alarmingly a few days earlier, were rather wary of the liner's similarly constructed superstructure and preferred to muster below decks. Their attitude changed somewhat when it was pointed out that the watertight doors were even more of a potential hazard in the event of an attack. On June 3, orders were received for the ship to return to Southampton and bring the survivors home. Many of the crew were disappointed at this as they were fully prepared for a couple of months away, and felt strongly that they hadn't really participated as much as they could have done. Many were annoyed that the Canberra had been allowed to do so much more.

The QE2 arrived back in Southampton on June 11 to a tumultuous welcome. The ship had succeeded in bringing the majority of 5th Brigade to the war zone within two weeks, and had steamed a total of 14,967 miles. She was greeted by the Queen Mother, dressed in blue and standing on the after deck of the royal yacht Britannia. She paid the following message of tribute to the ship that had

upheld the war record of the Cunard Queens so well:

"I am pleased to welcome you back as the QE2 returns to home waters after your tour of duty in the South Atlantic. The exploits of your own ship's company and the deeds of valour of those who served in Antelope, Ardent and Coventry have been acclaimed throughout the land and I am proud to add my personal tribute."

***Arriving back in Southampton on June 11, 1982 (Peter Boyd-Smith photo)***

# XII The New Cunarder for the 21st Century

THe QE2's arrival in Southampton on October 25, 1986 was a milestone in Cunard history, as it signalled the end of the steam era which had lasted for 146 years. The line's Britannia had been the first ship to establish a regular transatlantic steamship service, and the same company's QE2 had ended it. The next scheduled voyage would be under diesel power following a refit costing around £100 million.

The life expectancy of a transatlantic liner is estimated at around thirty years. The QE2 had been in service for just seventeen when Cunard decided that a major refit was essential – for cost effectiveness and longevity. They were looking to the future and wanted to ensure that the ship would continue to sail beyond the thirty year mark and into the 21st century. The choice was between building a new comparable ship, or upgrading an existing one with an already enviable reputation. They chose the latter, as £100 million was still three times less than that required to commission and build a similar vessel.

Consequently, in summer 1983, Cunard invited well known shipyards and diesel engine manufacturers from all over the world to Southampton for a meeting where each was introduced to the plan to upgrade the QE2. This was largely to obtain information about conversion time and estimated price. Many of the shipyards were apparently unwilling to accept the fact that Cunard wanted the ship withdrawn from service for just seven months for the work to be undertaken. Others had unrealistic ideas: Japanese and Korean shipyards offered such cheap price tenders that Cunard didn't take them seriously. Furthermore, a Dutch yard and British shipbuilder group were said to have intimated that they didn't want the work, with reasons given ranging from lack of management to inadequate yard facilities. Following this, Cunard held discussions with Lloyd Werft in Bremerhaven, Blohm & Voss in Hamburg, and with Howaldtswerke in Hamburg and Kiel. The latter soon backed out. The remaining two yards prepared conversion specifications and late in the summer of 1985, Cunard made their decision to go with Lloyd Werft after a series of hard negotiations in Bremerhaven, London and New York. The contract was finally signed in London on October 24, 1985.

The ship entered the shipyard just over a year later on October 26, 1986, for 179 consecutive days to undergo the largest and most complicated conversion in civil merchant shipping history. The lead time was not particularly generous in view of the considerable preparation that was required for constructions, co-ordination work and material ordering to ensure that the schedule could be adhered to – there were stiff penalties if it wasn't!

***A new dawn for the QE2 (Author photo)***

Queen Elizabeth 2

Queen Elizabeth 2

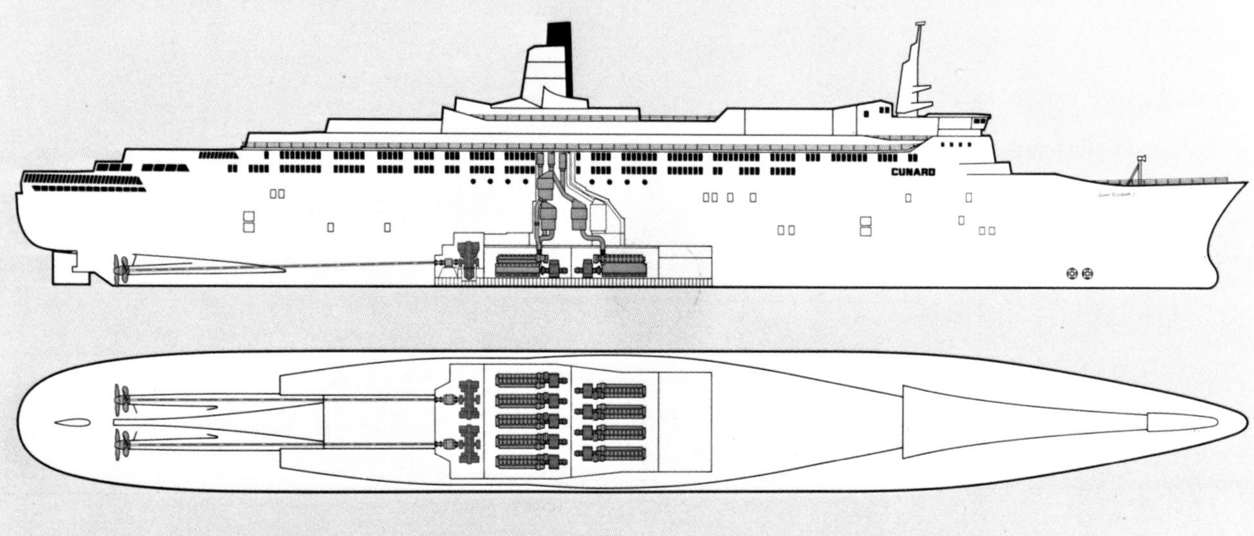


General arrangement of new propulsion plant
Nine 9L58/64 MAN B&W four-stroke Diesel engines
with a total output of 130.000 HP

***Cunard decided to upgrade the QE2 to diesel power (Man B & W photo)***

A project team was put together, which, on arrival of the ship numbered 35 engineers and technicians. In addition, Cunard was preparing its own project in parallel with the Germans. Initially a network plan was developed for time control, with a computer being used to govern costing. Using a plastic engine room model, the pipework and wiring were planned, designed and fabricated at a scale of 1:20.

Meanwhile, new components were being drawn from all over Europe, laying to rest the "British made" dominance of the earlier Cunard ships. The "new" QE2 would have German diesel generators and Dutch propellers – but still retain British propulsion motors. The lead year was filled with negotiations, discussions and technical problem solving. However, when the QE2 finally arrived, the Germans had completed all their preparations and the nearby sheds were full of new diesel engines, foundations, generators, propulsion motors, switchboards and piping systems. Manpower was fully taken care of, and to ease the pressure on Lloyd Werft, allied shipyards had placed some of their labour at the company's disposal.

Many aficionados were sad to see the passing of steam as propulsion, but it was a sign of the times and diesel was already being used, at least in part, in almost every other cruise ship afloat. Added to this, Cunard had been experiencing difficulties for some time in obtaining spares for the QE2's Pamatrada turbines, which were rapidly becoming obsolete. What was even more important was that the turbines had become very expensive to run, especially following the considerable oil price increases of the seventies. By converting the ship to diesel, Cunard would save a third in fuel costs and also be able to run the QE2 at a faster service speed if they so wished. However, it is noteworthy that the liner's steam turbine engines were of a design far ahead of their time when originally conceived; the Queen Mary needed 24 boilers; the Queen Elizabeth, 12, whilst the QE2 had performed comparably with only three.

A press conference followed the QE2's arrival at Bremerhaven and then the countdown began. The funnel was dismantled, casings opened, and five

***One of the Man B & W diesel engines under test at Augsburg during the one year lead time that Cunard afforded the project (Man B & W photo)***

weeks after the commencement of work, some 4,700 tons of scrap materials from the ship's engine rooms lay on the quayside. This included the ship's three main boilers, two main turbines, three auxiliary turbines for electrical power generation, both propeller shaft units, together with considerable pipes and minor equipment.

Because the new machinery had to be installed in the existing hull, it was necessary to remove and replace parts of the load bearing structures – thus weakening the hull. In order to overcome this problem, a plan was devised so that the re-installation of new bearing members was performed just before the stripping out of the old parts took place. These new sections were planned in close co-operation with Lloyd's shipping register officials in collaboration with advanced computer systems.

Whilst this was going on, the ship was opened in several locations – the main access ways were to the boiler and turbine casings, but further openings were cut into the ship's sides below the waterline, as well as into the aft part of the propeller shaft areas on both port and starboard sides. The computerized planning had allowed six weeks for the strip out, but everything took more time than estimated, and difficulties were unavoidably encountered in getting some of the machinery loose, together with problems of several minor fires. All this resulted in a delay of seven days and really began to put the pressure on Lloyd Werft.

The major operation of removing and refitting the QE2's power plant was far from straightforward because the arrangement of the lower decks was designed for turbines, not diesels. Consequently, the German engineers were faced with considerable problems relating to the angle and length of shafts, as well as engine configuration. In addition, space had to be found for the new reduction gear components. These problems were solved by using a system of electrical linkages which meant that the generators themselves could be sited almost anywhere in the old boiler-room. All this led to the myriad of lagged pipes, which had been a feature of the old boiler-room, being ripped out to be replaced with electrical connections and cables. It would all amount to faster starting and stopping as well as almost instantaneous full astern power – or so they hoped.

One of the first tasks was the replacement of the propellers and shafts in dry dock. The new set were significantly more advanced than those that they replaced for several reasons. First was that they were controllable pitch (CP). This provides the bridge with the facility to adjust the angle of the propeller blades to such an extent that astern propulsion can be created whilst the shaft continues to rotate normally. Added to this, the shape of the blades themselves had also undergone a metamarphosis and had become much more curved than before – technically known as highly skewed, to such an extent that the blades almost overlap each other. This feature assists engine economy and also has the effect of reducing wear on the propellers themselves. Substantial model tests were carried out before the final propeller decisions were made, even to the extent that different shapes of the QE2's bulbous bow were tested. Following the results of these experiments, it was decided that the bow would be retained and five bladed propellers of 5.8 metres in diameter, weighing 42 tons would be used, each driven by a 44 MW main propulsion motor of approx. 60,000 horsepower.

However, the propeller technology didn't end there, and a Hamburg professor named E.H. Otto Grim took responsibility for two strange wheels that were fitted, one to each of the new propellers, on the same shaft. These new devices made use of backwash propeller turbulence created when the ship was underway – turbulence that, until then, had been completely wasted, but was now converted to a fuel saving of up to four per-cent. The Grim wheels, as they became known, revolve at around 35 per-cent of the powered propeller and feature nine blades which look like long wobbly vanes, all of a larger diameter than the ships main five bladed screws. Its diameter is about 15 to 20 per-cent larger than the propeller that it is paired with. In addition to the fuel saving, Cunard were hoping for improved manoeuvring and better ship-stopping times. They calculated that the actual cost of installing Grim wheels was small compared to the ongoing saving resulting from increased output and decreased fuel requirement.

With the ship's distinctive funnel standing on the Bremerhaven dockside, the QE2 had lost her identity, albeit temporarily. The removal was necessary because it provided the only practical means of access to the engine rooms, revealing a huge shaft. With the engine rooms just gaping empty caverns it was time to put the two General Electric Company motors into position. These each weighed 350 tons and were handled by HEBE 2, an enormous floating crane with a lifting capacity of some 1,600 tons, normally used in conjunction with oil rig servicing. The nine MAN-B & W diesel/generators combined, each as big as a double decker bus, were craned into place. After these came the switchboards, all lifted into the chimney-like hole through eleven of the QE2's decks. March 1987 saw all the new machinery safely in position.

The nine diesels installed in the ship were medium speed MAN B & W four stroke type 9L 58/64 units with a designed capacity each of 10.625 KW at 400 RPM, anti-vibration mounted. GEC supplied 10.5 MW output 10 KV/60 cycle generators which were rigid mounted to the QE2's foundations, with connection to the diesel unit made in each case through flexible Vulcan couplings. GEC also supplied the synchronous propeller motors, each of 44 MW at 144 RPM, directly fed from the 10 KV main switchboard. Two synchro-converters were also fitted for start-up of propeller motors and for manoeuvring runs at 72 RPM, with all the electric power supply to the ship achieved through the 10 KV main switchboards, then 10 KV/3.3 KV step-down transformers into 3.3 KV/415 volt transformers. The total capacity installed added up to 95,625 KW, which is equivalent to some 130,000 HP. This gave provision for about 88 MW to the propulsion motors, which combined to provide the upgraded QE2 with a potential service speed exceeding 33 knots. However, what was of paramount importance for Cunard was the fuel consumption which was reduced to almost half that required by the old turbine plant. Post-conversion voyages would see the ship using just 270 tons daily at service speed as opposed to the 600 tons or so that the turbines had gobbled for 17 years at 28.5 knots.

The exhaust air and gas pipes from the nine diesels were built into a framework structure having an overall depth of 35 metres and weighing about 250 tons. All the exhaust pipes within the stack were anti-vibration mounted using spring elements to ensure isolation from the stack structure itself. In fact the main unit has a rigid connection to the QE2 only at the level of the signal deck, as the fewer

*The removal of the funnel was necessary because it provided the only practical means of access to the engine rooms. Through the gaping hole, the diesel engines and motors were lowered (Man B & W photo)*

connections made, the less chance of unwanted vibrations being transmitted into the passenger areas.

As we all know, the QE2 is famous for its funnel, but the once proud structure that now stood

***The engine control console has a mimic diagram of the complete generation, distribution and electric propulsion system (Cunard photo)***

on the dockside was not of sufficient size to house the nine new exhaust pipes, and so a new design was required. Cunard were at pains to ensure that it retained, as closely as possible, the shape of the original funnel. However, an additional 55 metres of outlet surface had to be created for machinery supply and exhaust air. Discussions took place between the shipyard and Cunard who both

***The QE2 was given a new, fatter funnel (Author photos)***

presented their wishes through several models. This lead to the testing of a wooden ship in a wind tunnel, allowing a simulation of many operating situations to be created, and providing a photographic record of exhaust gas flow by using white smoke on the model. The final design closely resembled that of the original, except that it is somewhat thicker and chunkier. The casual observer would not perceive any alterations, save perhaps for a more emphasised marking of the characteristic Cunard colours.

Vibration was a potential problem with the new engines, as diesel is more prone to this problem than steam, and Lloyd Werft were under contractual orders from Cunard to ensure that this was minimized. The contract actually stated that "vibration under diesel-electric power may not exceed that registered during the turbine era". For this reason, the Bremerhaven engineers travelled on part of the ship's last steam-based world cruise and made careful measurements of vibration at various different speeds. Their concern in the new power system centralized on two principal areas – turbulence beneath the stern caused by propellers, and sympathetic resonance from the engines throughout the vessel. Consequently, Lloyd Werft were very careful to ensure that adequate sound insulation was installed with the new machinery, and in addition to conventional planning against sound and fire, extra hi-tech sound treatments were added underneath six deck transverse bulkheads, and also the outer longitudinal walls between six deck and seven deck. Added to this, all ventilation inlets and outlets were fitted with large silencers, with much of the main machinery anti-vibration mounted in the hull.

Whilst the re-engining was proceeding, considerable work was being carried out throughout the interior of the ship. Another eight penthouse suites, equipped with balconies, electrically adjustable beds, built-in television sets, video recorders and gold bathroom fittings, were placed on the signal deck. In addition, the corridors and staircase serving the penthouses were completely converted, and despite limited space, wall and deckhead panellings of art deco styling were installed, producing a very rich atmosphere in keeping with the accommodation.

Due to the installation of the new rooms, the Queen's Grill restaurant, reserved exclusively for penthouse passengers, had to be enlarged. However the original feel of the room was maintained, and a gold leaf ceiling, cream coloured leather chairs and black covered banquette seating with maple veneer combines to achieve the expensive, elegant effect that Cunard desired. Meanwhile, the Queen's Grill lounge had its bar re-built and all the seating renewed.

Lloyd Werft extended the shopping arcade too. It was made 16 metres longer and also entirely converted to feature display units arranged in cubicles sections, filled with shops such as Louis Ferraud, Louis Vitton, Christian Dior, H. Stern, Gucci and Dunhill. Chromium and maple balustrades combine towards the nearby double room which has been renamed the grand lounge. In fact, from the forward part of the shopping arcade there is now a half-round double-sided stairway leading down into what used to be the double down room. This stairway provides the background for the bandstand which is built with a retractable, sectioned stage. The new staircase was to have a dual role – passenger convenience and also as a feature for cabaret shows. The walls in this large room, the ship's entertainments centre, utilise bird's eye maple and white laminate, with floors arranged in three levels to enable clear sight lines to the stage from the 500 red and blue leather covered armchairs arranged in groups around small glass tables. The double down bar aft is transformed to offer a cheerful pub-like atmosphere by day, and provides an "intimate spot for evening relaxation". New doors will provide access to deck, where passengers will find an array of sports activities. When I first visited the room in the summer of 1988, I was most impressed with the unique ceiling which features "starlight panel lighting", where literally thousands of tiny recessed bulbs twinkle, creating the feeling of being outside under a clear night sky.

Attached to the grand lounge on the starboard side is the teen centre, whilst the adult centre is opposite to port. In the teen centre can now be found a large television set, video games, a juke box, table tennis, air hockey and a dance floor. Cunard call it "the perfect place for mingling, dancing and enjoying soft drinks". The adult centre is rather more restrained with a reading corner and several card tables together with table shuffleboard, chess, backgammon, disc pool and video facilities.

At the aft end of the Grand Lounge, downstairs

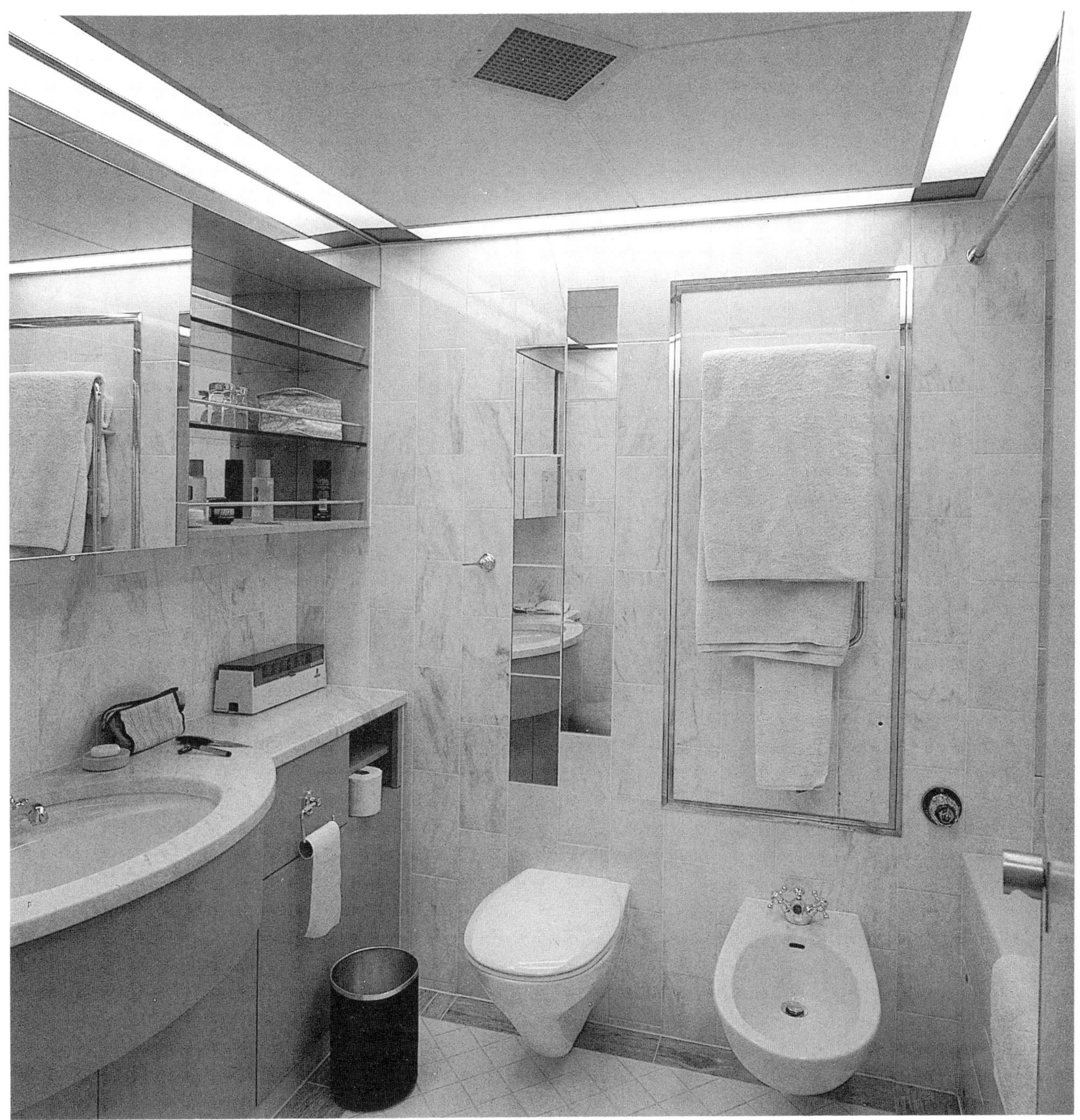

***Interiors of the completed new penthouses with Art Deco overtones (P.A. Kroehnert photo courtesy of Platou Ship Design)***

between the teen and adult centres, there is the yacht club bar. This was completely converted and extended to incorporate the aft corridor facing towards the outdoor sports area. A maritime impression is created here with a wave shaped ceiling construction, yacht models, posters and photographs, plus a unique transparent glazed piano with a drink rail incorporated into the design, and bar stools arranged around the piano casing. The club also sports a new veneered wood bar counter.

The outdoor sporting area aft of the yacht club

***The Queens grill, reserved for penthouse passengers, had to be enlarged (P.A. Kroehnert photo courtesy of Cunard)***

was also fully converted and now has an automatic golfing unit, two shuffleboard fields and a multi-functional centre part with provisions for basketball, badminton, paddle tennis and punchball as well as golf driving facilities. In fact, the automatic golf unit is the first of its kind ever fitted on a ship. It simulates famous courses in the world and allows electronic measurement and evaluation of golf shots based on speed, angle and direction. A screen indicates where the ball would have actually fallen on a given golf course, projections of 900 course pictures being available, with a computer simultaneously providing a readout of shot length.

***Lloyd Weft extended the shopping arcade (P.A. Kroehnert photo courtesy of Cunard)***

Christian Dior

***The rear of the shopping arcade above the double down room, renamed the grand lounge (Author photo)***

If one leaves the Grand Lounge at its forward end on the starboard side, the theatre bar is approached, which has several display cases near it, one of which houses a display of maritime memorabilia provided by Cobwebs Ocean Liner shop in Southampton, whilst on the port side is a photographic display which leads into the casino bar. These two areas, along with the lido bar, were the only public rooms that were not upgraded or converted. Moving further forward you arrive at the Tables of the World restaurant, which has had almost £2 million spent on it, and is now known as the Mauretania. New wall panels and ceilings in the art deco style of the thirties are now featured, together with ceilings with decorative suspended mirror squares. The restaurant is split into two sections, and fitted to the wall of the smaller one of the two is an oil painting of the old four-funnelled Mauretania steamship.

Underneath the Mauretania restaurant are the Princess grill and Columbia restaurants. Both have been given upgrades, with the Princess grill still reached through a spiral staircase from its burgundy leather bar on one deck. Aft of the Columbia restaurant, on the quarter deck, is the Queen's Room. The original fibreglass chairs have been replaced by box-shaped leather armchairs, which now contrast the upturned white trumpet columns that still remain from the original design. It houses 250 passengers seated around a large dance floor. The room can now be divided with sliding doors to form a central part and two verandahs if required. Adjacent to the Queen's room at the aft end are fitted two eight metre long buffet units, then further aft is the unchanged club lido and the magradome. In fact, Lloyd Werft were responsible for the

***The stage of the new grand lounge – note the starlight panel lighting! (P.A. Kroehnert photo courtesy of Cunard)***

***For the less energetic there is the relaxed atmosphere of the card room (Author photo)***

***The Princess Grill (Author photo)***

conversion of this too, back in 1983. Down on one deck, the outdoor pool area has been provided with new teak decking and two whirlpools plus children's paddling pool. In addition, the main pool has new

***The Columbia restaurant houses Samuel Cunard's commemorative silver cup (Author photo)***

tiling, and the whole area provided with upgraded deck chairs and sun shade tables. Passengers preferring informal lunch here are able to enjoy complimentary hot dogs and hamburgers all day, as well as choose from a full service bar.

***General view of the Columbia restaurant (P.A. Kroehnert photo courtesy of Cunard)***

***The club lido/magradome, which Lloyd Weft converted in 1983, has become one of the most popular on the whole ship (Author photo)***

The enormous kitchens on the QE2 were given an entire conversion with new equipment being installed throughout. In addition, the midship's lobby, the main passenger entrance area, now features a more contemporary appearance with new wall decorations, a ceiling with concentric mirror elements, plus a revised seating group in its lowered circular central part. The bright green leather has thankfully been replaced by restrained white upholstery, matching the similarly coloured grand piano which is played softly as passengers embark or disembark. This has the effect of producing a very relaxing, quiet atmosphere, and I found myself easily able to speak to fellow passengers here, without having to raise my voice above intrusive taped music.

The already popular IBM computer learning centre is a new installation, now located adjacent to the forward lobby, where training courses are on offer on 14 computer terminals. There are separate sections now for passengers wishing to work

***Adjacent to the magradome is a fully equipped disco – the floor lights up in coloured squares at night (Author photo)***

***The outdoor pool area has been provided with new teak decking, two whirlpools and a children's paddling pool (Author photo)***

independently, and an extensive range of software is stored in the room. Whilst on the subject of hi-tech, greater use of television is now made throughout the ship, and passengers will be able to view world news, sport and educational programmes, as well as accessing information on shipboard facilities, services and programming. In addition, throughout all the public rooms, alleyways, staircases and to many of the passenger cabins, new carpets have been fitted, 27,000 square metres in all were removed. Also, for the first time on a ship, Cunard is introducing a shipboard evening dress service, offering men the latest in formal wear for rent or purchase, thereby simplifying packing for the voyage. A new boardroom will cater for executives interested in private conferences or small meetings, with a flexible design that can easily be adjusted to accommodate private cocktail parties and dinners, as well as acting as a quiet room for reading and working.

When the QE2 re-entered service to a fanfare of fireworks and ships sirens, she was almost a completely new ship. Her first westbound crossing was deservedly dubbed a second maiden voyage. Now Cunard once again had a vessel that exceeded passenger requirements and provided a 21st century example of the memorable years of the transatlantic Queens.

# Appendix

## Comparative Statistics

***Queen Elizabeth 2***
Owned by Cunard Line Ltd.
Port of registry: Southampton.
Classification society: Lloyd's Register of Shipping
Built by: John Brown & Co. Shipyard (Clydebank) Ltd.
Entered service: May 1968.
Principal particulars:
Length o.a.: 963 feet.
Length btw. prp. 885 feet.
Breadth 104 feet.
Designed draught: 32 ft.
Gross tonnage 66,451.
Net tonnage 38,243.
Depth from keel to funnel: 204 feet.
Depth from keel to signal mast: 205 feet.
Special features of new engines:
Having 130,000 hp this is the largest non-military used ship propulsion plant with the two largest electric driving engines in the world.
Largest controllable pitch propeller plant with Grim wheels.

***Technical data before conversion***
Main propulsion plant: 2x John Brown Eng. steam turbines.
Propellers: 2 x 6 bladed fixed propellers 5.80 diameter.
Output at propellers: 2 x 55,000 hp.
Boilers: 3 x Foster Wheeler.
Bow thrusters: 2 x Stone KaMeWa 1,000 hp each.
Stabilizers: 4 x Denny Brown.
Fresh water: 3 x H.P. evap's.
Generators: 400 tons/day each.

***Tank capacities***
Fresh water: 4,201 tons.
Fuel oil: 6,425 tons.
Ballast water: 3,724.

***Technical data after conversion***
Main propulsion plant: 9 x 9L 58/64 M.A.N. – B & W diesel units.
Propellers: 2 x 5 bladed C.P. propellers, 5.80 m diameter; 2 Grim wheels 6.7 m diameter.
Output at propellers: 2 x 44 MW.
Boilers: 9 x Sunrod exhaust gas boilers; 2 x Sunrod donkey boilers.
Fresh water: 4 x Serck.
Generators: vacuum evaporators, 250 tons each; 1 x reverse osmosis 450 tons/day.

***Tank capacities***
Fresh water: 2,534 tons.

Fuel oil: 4,640 tons.
Ballast water: 4,617 tons.

### *Queen Elizabeth*

Length overall: 1031 feet.
Length on waterline: 1004 feet.
Beam: 118 feet.
Depth moulded to promenade deck: 92 feet 6 inches.
Length of promenade deck: 724 feet.
Keel to top of superstructure: 132 feet.
Keel to forward funnel: 184 feet.
Keel to masthead: 234 feet.
Draught: 39 feet 6½ inches.
Gross tonnage: 83,673.
Service speed: 28½ knots.
Number of decks: 13.
Lifts: 24.
Passenger capacity: 2082.
Officers and crew: 1190.
Cargo space: 212,105 cubic feet.
Main engines: four sets of single reduction geared turbines with 257,000 blades, developing 160,000 shaft horsepower to drive four propellers of 18 feet in diameter and weighing 32 tons each.
Boilers: 12 large water tube boilers burning oil fuel, supplying steam to main engines at a pressure of 425 lbs per square inch at a temperature of 750 degrees F.
Power stations: two, producing total power of 8,800 kw. There are 4000 miles of wiring, 30,000 lamps, 650 electric motors and 700 clocks.
Hull: Comprises 131 watertight compartments. Weight of metal 50,000 tons.
Funnels: 2 elliptical in shape, 44 feet fore and aft by 29 feet wide. The forward was 80 feet, and the aft 78 feet above the boat deck.
Rudder: 140 tons with doors for internal inspection.
Anchors: four – each being 16 tons, with 165 fathoms (990 feet) of chain cable – links of cable were two feet in length and the total weight was 300 tons.

### *Queen Mary*

Length overall: 1019 feet 6 inches.
Length of waterline: 1004 feet.
Beam: 118 feet.
Depth moulded to promenade deck: 92 feet 6 inches.
Length of promenade deck: 724 feet.
Keel to top of superstructure: 124 feet.
Keel to forward funnel: 181 feet.
Keel to masthead: 237 feet.
Draught: 39 feet 4½ inches.
Gross tonnage: 81,237.
Service speed: 28½ knots.
Number of decks: 12.
Lifts: 20.
Passenger capacity: 1948.
Officers and crew: 1174.
Cargo space: 152,600 cubic feet.
Main engines: 4 sets of single reduction geared turbines developing 160,000 shaft horsepower to drive four propellers, each 18 feet in diameter and weighing 32 tons. The four main gear wheels were 13½ feet in diameter with a total weight of 300 tons.
Boilers: 24 oil burning water tube boilers supplying steam to the main engines at a pressure of 400 lbs per square inch at a temperature of 700 degrees F. 3 double-ended aux. boilers. There were almost 160,000 tubes in the boiler installation, and the main steam piping was over 2,600 feet long.
Power stations: 2 – producing 9,100 kw. There were 520 motors totalling about 13,500 horsepower, plus nearly 700 clocks.
Hull: Comprises 151 watertight doors. Weight of metal was over 50,000 tons.
Funnels: 3 elliptical. 36 feet fore and aft by 23 feet 4 inches wide. Forward 70 feet 6 inches, middle 67 feet 6 inches and aft 62 feet 3 inches above the sun deck.
Rudder: 140 tons with doors for internal inspection.
Anchors: 3 anchors, each 16 tons with 165 fathoms (990 feet) of chain cable. Links of cable are two feet in length, with the total cable weight being over 200 tons.

# Index